CAREERS IN DEMAND
FOR HIGH SCHOOL GRADUATES

Public Safety
& Law

Daniel Lewis

MASON CREST

Mason Crest
450 Parkway Drive, Suite D
Broomall, PA 19008
www.masoncrest.com

Printed in the United States of America
First printing
9 8 7 6 5 4 3 2 1

Series ISBN: 978-1-4222-4132-5
Hardcover ISBN: 978-1-4222-4141-7

Library of Congress Cataloging-in-Publication Data is available on file.

Developed and Produced by Print Matters Productions, Inc.
(www.printmattersinc.com)
Cover and Interior Design by Lori S Malkin Design LLC

CAREERS IN DEMAND FOR HIGH SCHOOL GRADUATES

Agriculture, Food & Natural Resources

Armed Forces

Computers, Communications & the Arts

Construction & Trades

Fitness, Personal Care Services & Education

Health Care & Science

Hospitality & Human Services

Public Safety & Law

Sales, Marketing & Finance

Transportation & Manufacturing

KEY ICONS TO LOOK FOR:

 Words to understand: These words with their easy-to-understand definitions will increase the reader's understanding of the text while building vocabulary skills.

 Sidebars: This boxed material within the main text allows readers to build knowledge, gain insights, explore possibilities, and broaden their perspectives by weaving together additional information to provide realistic and holistic perspectives.

 Educational Videos: Readers can view videos by scanning our QR codes, providing them with additional educational content to supplement the text. Examples include news coverage, moments in history, speeches, iconic sports moments and much more!

 Text-dependent Questions: These questions send the reader back to the text for more careful attention to the evidence presented there.

 Research projects: Readers are pointed toward areas of further inquiry connected to each chapter. Suggestions are provided for projects that encourage deeper research and analysis.

CONTENTS

In the 1600s, Thomas Hobbes, a famous British philosopher, tried to imagine a world without rules, regulations, laws, or a government to enforce them. It seemed to him that the result would be a war of "all against all." Without a sense of safety or security, everyone would be haunted by the "continual fear, and danger of violent death; and the life of man, solitary, poor, nasty, brutish, and short." If this were not bad enough, human society was also threatened by natural disasters such as fires, floods, hurricanes, earthquakes, and epidemics.

In order to prevent chaos, governments make laws, and private businesses make rules and regulations. It is true that these enactments restrict individual freedom. However, no society could survive if everyone did whatever he or she wanted to do. Millions of jobs exist to support this system of laws, rules, and services to benefit the public good. People are at work day and night to make sure that other people remain safe. They keep terrorists off airplanes, arrest criminals, prevent fires, send ambulances to accident scenes, keep order in courtrooms, prevent fights in bars, and guard private businesses. These are the types of jobs highlighted in this volume on careers in public safety, law, and security.

The nice thing about a job or career in public safety is the knowledge that what you do makes a difference in someone's life and society as a whole. Public safety jobs prevent and treat crime, disease, and natural disasters. A store manager or a bank teller might wonder if his or her job has any meaning in the greater scheme of things. If you work in public safety, law, or security, you usually will not have that problem. You know that your work in protective services is crucial to the general well-being of society.

Most jobs categories in this field should continue to grow. Since the attack on the United States in 2001, fear of terrorism has led to an upsurge in security -related positions, such as transportation security officers (also known as airport security screeners). At the same time, crime and punishment remain growth industries in America. The United States has more people in prisons than any other country in the world. As of 2017, more than 2.3 million people were behind bars; the U.S. prison population has quadrupled since 1980. Because crime and natural disasters will probably never disappear, there will always be plenty of protection services careers from which to choose. If you decide to work in public safety, your skills will always be in demand.

Is a career in public safety, law, or security right for you? Many people go into these careers for the wrong reasons. Some want to boss people around or fire guns at "bad guys." Others have allowed television shows to convince them that the job is glamorous. Actually, most public safety and security jobs are preventive in nature and involve irregular hours and considerable risk. For example, around 80 or 90 firefighters die on the job every year. Even people who work as bouncers and bailiffs face very real physical danger, and even death, attempting to do their job. Many security jobs do not have regular hours and often involve night work.

Just as often, however, the rewards for working in public safety, law, and security are huge. Every safe day testifies to your hard work and dedication. You might not receive a hero's standing ovation at the end of every day, but your efforts will be appreciated, not the least by yourself. If you have an interest in protecting and helping people who are weak or vulnerable, then you might enjoy a career in this field.

A Range of Opportunity

This volume highlights eight careers in public safety, law, and security that are available at an entry level with only a high school diploma. Some of these jobs might be familiar and some unfamiliar. The range of careers in public safety is broad. This book examines the following:

- Law enforcement personnel protect the public's health, well-being, and property. This type of job includes detectives, animal control officers, and police officers.

- Security and protective service workers maintain the safety of buildings or objects. You might work as a transportation security officer, a security guard, or a nightclub bouncer.

- Emergency and fire management personnel might directly fight fires or work as dispatchers by taking emergency calls and sending help to the callers.

- Correctional officers guard people who have been arrested or are in jail or prison. Bailiffs represent a similar position; they keep order in a courtroom.

- Crime-scene cleaners work in the public health field. They clean, disinfect, and restore a crime scene site to its previous state.

Jobs with a High School Diploma or Less

Some of these careers in this volume, such as crime-scene cleaner or security guard, require little or no academic study or training beyond high school. Others, such as firefighter or police officer, require extensive training. Many public safety, law, and security careers are becoming increasingly complex. However, you don't need to spend four years in a classroom to learn these job skills. In many cases, you can learn additional required skills while you work on the job. Many employers offer certificate or apprenticeship programs to help their employees.

Occasionally, you may need to enroll in a specialized training program at a community college, trade school, or technical school. However, unlike a degree program, the training for these positions can often be completed in a few months. Once you start working, many employers will even pay for additional preparation. This allows you to advance your career while someone else pays the tuition for training.

It's true that some of these jobs, such as working in law enforcement, are difficult to break into with only a high school diploma. Even careers like firefighter and corrections officer are increasingly requiring more and more credentials at the entry level. High school students, however, can prepare for careers in public safety, law, and security in a variety of ways. Enrolling in language arts classes will help you gain the skills you need to communicate effectively, especially in written reports. Science classes may be helpful in certain fields, such as crime-scene cleaning.

There are other ways to gain skills and experience. Summer is a great time to add some gloss to your résumé. Put away the beach towels and try to find a paid—or even unpaid—internship. A relevant class at a community college, technical program, or career academy will also go a long way to help you get your first job in the field. Make sure you are physically fit; working as a firefighter, bouncer, or law enforcement officer requires you to be in top condition. If all else fails, acquiring a related position might be useful. For example, a part-time job as a security guard for a store in the mall might be a stepping-stone to a position as a deputy sheriff trainee.

Employers in any field, but especially public safety and security, want to see that you are responsible, dedicated, and community oriented. One way to show this is by volunteering at a local hospital, tutoring, coaching a sport, serving as a Big Brother or Big Sister, or performing other types of community service. It is even better if you can find a volunteer position that meshes with your chosen field. What better way is there to prepare to apply for a firefighter trainee position than to join a volunteer fire department? It gives you a good background into the profession and also shows that you are serious about firefighting. Some schools even offer academic credit for volunteer work.

Even though the job descriptions for different careers in public safety vary widely, they retain some characteristics in common. Whether you are a police officer walking a beat or a bailiff keeping order in a courtroom, you need to be a careful, detail-oriented, conscientious worker. Employers of entry-level workers often do not care about diplomas. They know that they can train workers exactly to their own specifications. What they do want to see is a sense of responsibility, a willingness to learn, and a show of enthusiasm. If you have those things, you can begin a successful career without completing four years of college.

Benefits to Entering the Workplace after High School

Of course, there is the matter of money. In general, higher education is linked to higher earnings. Over a lifetime, Americans with a college diploma earn more than those with only a high school diploma by a considerable margin. However, more than 1 million of the nation's 3.1 million high school graduates go directly into the workforce each year. If you're reading this book, you understand that doing something besides pursuing a college degree after high school makes sense for many people. College is expensive, and costs continue to rise much faster than inflation. Many people cannot afford the thousands of dollars needed to get a degree. Others don't want to spend the money for tuition and books if they're not sure what they want to study. Time spent working gives you the opportunity to try out a field that interests you. By actually working in the field, you will learn whether or not you want to pursue this career.

If you are passionate about helping others, have a real desire to guard, serve and protect, and enjoy a job with many challenges, then a career in public safety is for you. These jobs can be stressful, but you will often be helping to make the world a safer and more enjoyable place. There are few jobs that offer similar levels of inner fulfillment and personal satisfaction.

▲ Transportation security jobs are homeland security jobs; U.S. national security depends on agents doing them properly.

Police Officer

1

Protect the public from criminals and danger. Enforce the law. Hold a position of respect and authority.

WORDS TO UNDERSTAND

agility: describes the ability to move quickly and easily.

game warden: a person who supervises hunting and makes sure rules are followed.

pertinent: relevant.

People depend on police officers to protect their lives and property. Everyone thinks they know the job from watching movies and television. Yet police work is rarely as exciting as portrayed in popular culture. Some officers go an entire career without ever firing a gun in the line of duty.

Police officers patrol an assigned area in order to prevent crime. Their main job is to identify, pursue, and arrest suspected criminals. If someone calls for assistance, police officers are dispatched to investigate and help. Police officers also uphold laws about traffic rules, noise, disorderly conduct, and other activities that can disrupt order in a community.

As a police officer trainee, you will receive thorough training in law enforcement. At the end of a probationary period, ranging from six months to three years, you will become a regular police officer.

◀ Police academy cadets run together during a training exercise. Cadets participate in about 900 hours of law enforcement training, covering 42 topics that include policing in the community, laws of arrest, leadership and professional ethics, and traffic enforcement.

Is This the Right Job for You?

To find out if being a police officer is a good fit for you, read each of the following questions and answer "Yes" or "No."

Yes	No	1. *Do you enjoy working outdoors?*
Yes	No	2. *Could you handle a job that might threaten your physical safety?*
Yes	No	3. *Are you willing to work evening, night, weekend, and holiday shifts?*
Yes	No	4. *Do you consider yourself honest and reliable?*
Yes	No	5. *Can you maintain control of your emotions and keep personal feelings to yourself?*
Yes	No	6. *Can you learn and apply many rules, regulations, and laws?*
Yes	No	7. *Are you sensitive to others' feelings and needs?*
Yes	No	8. *Can you maintain alertness during stressful situations?*
Yes	No	9. *Are you physically fit?*
Yes	No	10. *Do you enjoy working with and meeting people?*

If you answered "Yes" to most of these questions, consider a career as a police officer. To find out more about this job, read on.

What's the Work Like?

When you finish your training, you will be a regular police officer. This means you will provide protective services, as well as prevent, detect, and investigate crimes. Police work often involves personal risk and requires good judgment in all situations.

Police officers perform many different tasks. However, their most basic job is to patrol an assigned area in order to prevent crime and enforce laws and regulations. Tasks vary in their level of danger. Pulling over speeding cars and enforcing

TALKING MONEY

Salaries for police officers vary a great deal depending on the particular job—pay can range from $30,000 to more than $100,000 per year, depending on the situation. Detectives and criminal investigators make the most, while patrol officers and game wardens make the least. According to 2016 data from the U.S. Bureau of Labor Statistics, the average salary is $61,600 per year. Benefits, such as vacation, sick leave, and medical insurance, are usually excellent.

traffic rules, for example, can be relatively safe work. Officers may also have to search people, vehicles, property, and places. This requires having a basic conception of U.S. constitutional law. Many police departments now practice community policing. Officers build relationships with the people who live in local neighborhoods. By interacting with the community, police officers help enlist the public in fighting crime.

Another basic task is to respond to calls for help or emergency service. This may involve assisting people in need, identifying and arresting people, or even actively pursuing suspects. You may have to restrain and control resisting suspects and, in extreme cases, use firearms and other weapons. All these tasks require the ability to establish and keep control in explosive situations.

Police officers also investigate crimes, suspicious persons, and complaints. They collect and preserve evidence, search for missing people, question suspects, and interview witnesses.

▲ Although most traffic stops are nonviolent, police officers must take precautions. Police officers often stand behind the pillar that separates the two side windows, behind the driver, in case they approach a dangerous person with a firearm or other weapon.

You might have to testify or present evidence in a court proceeding.

The responsibilities of a police officer are extremely broad and are not limited to the duties mentioned above. Police must respond in some way to all situations that may occur while they are on duty. In fact, part of the appeal of a job as a police officer is the wide range of work experiences. However, in large police departments, officers may be assigned to a specific type of duty.

TALKING TRENDS

The crime rate and the economy go up and down. These two factors influence the hiring of police officers. Therefore, the number of law enforcement jobs varies from year to year and from place to place. In general, the number of police officers should grow at an average rate through 2024, according to the Bureau of Labor Statistics. Fear of terrorism and concern about crime help keep the demand for police services steady.

Who's Hiring?

- Local governments (Cities employ about four out of every five police officers.)
- State governments (Police officers known as state troopers arrest criminals and patrol highways.)

Where Are the Jobs?

Positions as a police officer can be found throughout the United States. In 2016, police officers held more than 800,000 jobs, according to the Bureau of Labor Statistics. However, the majority of positions are in large cities and suburbs, simply because most of the people live there. Police departments are usually organized into districts. Officers patrol a specific area in the district. As a police officer, you may work alone or with a partner, on foot, in a car, or even on a bicycle or on horseback. Police officers try to become familiar with their patrol area and remain alert for anything unusual.

Police officers work in a variety of environments. They have to cope with many perils in their job. They face unpredictable situations, work in extreme weather conditions, and deal with hazardous substances. It is definitely not a job for everyone.

NOTES FROM THE FIELD

Police cadet, Bend, Oregon

Q: *How did you get your job?*

A: I got started in the program because of a friend who was in it. I didn't even know it existed until he told me about it, and then I asked the school's resource officer to give me more information. After talking about it for a while, he said I would be a good candidate, and a few days later I picked up an application at the police department. A few months [later] I was called back, as they hire yearly, and was scheduled for an interview. One of the better points that I had on my résumé was my activities for the JROTC [Junior Reserve Officers Training Corps] unit I was in at the time, which shows great commitment and maturity.

Q: *What do you like best about your job?*

A: The best part of the job is making a difference at the end of the day. If you can help a few people or improve someone's day, then [that is] my favorite part of the job. Although most of the time will be spent training for competitions and for a career as a law enforcement agent, it still feels good to know that you might use these skills later as a sworn officer. If you want to be a police officer, nothing is better: you are in patrol cars, get to talk to officers constantly, and just be in that world to a much higher degree than the average person as well as gaining a lot of experience to help you later in life.

Q: *What's the most challenging part of the job?*

A: The police cadet program I am in is mostly training. When we have a meeting, we go over whatever topic is on the docket for the night, whether it be felony traffic stops, courtroom testimony, or building searches. All of it is taught by police officers from the department and is hands-on. Otherwise, when riding with the officers, you are mostly just an assistant, jotting down notes and being another set of eyes. However, as you ascend through the ranks you can gain more privileges when riding with an officer, from doing all the radio work to operating the MDT [mobile data terminal, used to communicate with the central dispatch office]. When we have an event going on, such as a concert or parade, we are the security for the event. Often we block off traffic, meet with the public to make sure everything is going all right for them, and if there are any disturbances, we are the first to arrive. It is one of the more exciting parts of this particular job and gives you a lot of experience in dealing with people when you are a representative of the city.

Q: *What are the keys to success to being a police officer?*

A: My best advice would be to not get into any legal trouble. You can almost count yourself out if you have anything more than a traffic ticket, and even that will be a detriment to you being accepted. Otherwise, take **pertinent** classes in school to show you are genuinely interested in the field. Once again, I stress the value of a JROTC program of any type; it gives you more experience in following and giving orders than any other class, and is probably the most valuable thing I took away from high school.

Police officers usually work 40-hour weeks, but paid overtime is very common. Officers have to work different shifts because the police must provide protection around the clock. New employees often work weekends, holidays, and nights. In most places in the United States, police officers are expected to be armed and to be prepared to apply their authority whether on or off duty. One of the keys to the job is to maintain alertness in extreme conditions, particularly when preceded by long periods of boredom or relatively low stress.

A Typical Day

Here are some highlights of a typical day for a police officer.

Patrol the neighborhood. You are responsible for the security of people and property in your district. When you are extremely visible and observant, you help prevent crime.

▲ Although many police officers patrol in vehicles or on foot, some situations, especially in larger cities, call for patrol on bicycle or even horseback.

Write a report. This is the least glamorous part of police work. No matter what you do or where you work, you will have to write reports and maintain careful records. These will be needed if there is ever a court case involving your actions.

Respond to a traffic accident. You may have to direct traffic at the scene of an accident, give first aid, collect evidence and witnesses, or call for emergency equipment. Police officers also

▲ Police officers walk a beat in their district of Montrose, California.

enforce traffic and parking laws, check vehicle registration, follow suspicious vehicles, and assist stranded motorists.

Start Preparing Now

- Take some college-level classes. There is usually stiff competition for police officer jobs. People with some training in police science, criminal justice, or law enforcement have a huge edge.

- Make sure you are physically fit. Many law enforcement positions require strength, stamina, and **agility**. Can you cope?

- Learn to use firearms. You may never use a gun as a police officer, but you will need to know how. It is usually helpful to learn this skill on your own.

Training and How to Get It

A police officer's job is challenging. It involves a great deal of personal responsibility. Before your first assignment, you will usually go through a period of training. In state and large local police departments, new officers receive training in their own agency's police academy. This training might take three or four months. In small agencies, recruits might attend a regional or state academy.

Police officer training obviously includes classroom instruction in federal, state, and local laws. A career in law enforcement begins with knowing the law. You would also receive training in patrol, traffic control, the use of firearms, self-defense, first aid, and emergency response. Instructors also teach use-of-force policies, sensitivity and communications skills, crowd-control techniques, and the use of law enforcement equipment. A good training program will include hands-on experience with a veteran officer.

Watch an interview about what's required to be a police officer.

Police officer trainees usually become eligible for promotion after a probationary period ranging from six months to three years. In a large department, an officer may be able to train to become a detective or to specialize in a single type of police work, such as working with juveniles.

▲ New York City Police Department trainees salute at their graduation ceremony held at Madison Square Garden. Each year, the academy has two graduating classes. In October 2017, the NYPD welcomed 434 new officers at the graduation ceremony.

Learn the Lingo

Here are a few words to know as a police officer:

- **APB** An all points bulletin. An APB is broadcast to several law enforcement agencies. It contains information about a suspect who is to be investigated or arrested. An all points bulletin is sometimes known as a "BOLO," which stands for "be on the lookout."

- **CCW** Someone carrying a concealed weapon.

- **Gun run** A search for a weapon that was reportedly sighted in the hands of a "perp."

- **Obs** Short for "observation." The term is meant as a compliment for a police officer's ability to notice something that is not easily seen by others.

- **Perp** A perpetrator or criminal.

- **Rabbit** A fleeing subject.

Finding a Job

You can get information about becoming a police officer from local, state, and federal law enforcement agencies. You usually have to be at least 18 years old and sometimes as old as 21. Most police departments require at least a high school diploma. Candidates usually have to be U.S. citizens and meet strict physical and personal qualifications. Exams for police positions often include tests of vision, hearing, strength, and agility.

Most police positions are controlled by civil service regulations. In order to be appointed, you will have to take a written examination. Senior officers will then interview all candidates. Agencies also check out applicants' backgrounds. In some police departments, a psychologist interviews candidates or gives them a personality test. Most applicants also have to take lie detector or drug tests.

Police departments in some large cities hire high school graduates who are still in their teens as police officer trainees. For one or two years, they do office work and attend classes. When they reach the minimum age requirement, they may be appointed to the regular force.

Tips for Success

- Police work is a very social job. It is not all about shooting guns and fighting criminals. The best police officers establish and keep good relationships with their superiors, coworkers, and the public. You will have to be able to work independently and as a member of a team.

- Have a thick skin. People respond in various ways to police officers, sometimes negatively. Keep in mind that they are seeing the uniform first instead of the individual inside it. Don't take these reactions personally.

Reality Check

Police work can be very stressful and dangerous. Police officers need to be constantly alert and ready to deal with threatening situations. Law enforcement officers work in emotional situations. They often witness the death and suffering that result from accidents and crimes. A career in law enforcement can lead to depression.

Related Jobs to Consider

Correctional officer. A correctional officer guards and supervises inmates in a prison or jail. It's a law enforcement job with more routine work.

Security guard. Security guards are sometimes confused with the police because of similar uniforms and behaviors. However, a security guard's power comes from a private contract, not from the government.

Private detective or investigator. These jobs are similar to police work in that they involve collecting evidence and information, and conducting investigations and surveillance.

How to Move Up

- Take some training courses. Continuing training helps police officers improve their job performance. Officers are usually promoted to corporal, sergeant, lieutenant, and captain based on a written exam and on-the-job performance.

- Get an advanced degree. People with degrees receive higher salaries. Many police departments pay part or all of the tuition for officers to work toward degrees in criminal justice, police science, or public administration.

- Specialize. Some police officers specialize in fields such as chemical analysis, firearms instruction, or handwriting and fingerprint identification. Others work with special units, such as horseback or bicycle patrol, canine corps, special weapons and tactics (SWAT), or emergency response teams.

LEARN MORE ONLINE

INTERNATIONAL UNION OF POLICE ASSOCIATIONS
The IUPA is an AFL-CIO union for police officers. The Web site has a good collection of law enforcement links. http://www.iupa.org

NATIONAL ASSOCIATION OF POLICE ORGANIZATIONS
NAPO is a group of U.S. police unions and associations that works as a special interest group for law enforcement officers. NAPO provides information about current issues of interest to police officers. http://www.napo.org

NATIONAL SHERIFFS' ASSOCIATION
NSA is not just for sheriffs but for all law enforcement personnel. This site has lots of good general information on law enforcement. http://www.sheriffs.org

POLICE FOUNDATION
This organization, founded in 1970, was a pioneer of the community-policing concept. The Web site contains interesting research material. http://www.policefoundation.org

TEXT-DEPENDENT QUESTIONS

1. *About how many police officers are there in the United States?*

2. *What is an APB?*

3. *What are some tips for success in this job?*

4. *What are alternative jobs you might consider?*

RESEARCH PROJECTS

1. *To get a better sense of what this job is like, there are many memoirs you can read, such as:* 406: Officer Needs Assistance *by Raymond Petersen,* Bright Lights, Dark Places *by Debra Gauthier, and* NYPD Green *by Luke Waters. Your school librarian may have additional suggestions.*

2. *Choose one of the specialties listed above (such as chemical analysis or firearms instruction) and find out more about it. What is the job like? What additional training is needed?*

Court Bailiff

2

Be part of the judicial process. Take care of juries.
Ensure court safety.

WORDS TO UNDERSTAND

deadlocked: describes a situation in which no progress can be made.

magnetometer: device that can measures magnetic forces; used in security to detect metal.

overwrought: agitated.

repossessed: taken away because payments have not been made.

In the United States, court bailiffs—also known as marshals or court officers—are law enforcement officers who maintain safety and order in courtrooms. There are nearly 18,000 bailiffs in the United States; they enforce courtroom rules, assist judges, guard juries from outside contact, deliver court documents, and provide general security for courthouses. Bailiffs may escort witnesses in murder cases or advise people who have had their cars **repossessed.** Outside the courtroom, they may work delivering warrants, summonses, and orders to pay money owed (such as alimony). Some bailiffs work for private agencies, delivering eviction notices or repossessing cars. As with many law enforcement jobs, a bailiff career can be dangerous because it can involve dealing with people who are angry, unstable, or desperate.

◀ **Court bailiffs facilitate a prison transport for a man after a court hearing.**

Is This the Right Job for You?

To find out if being a court bailiff is a good fit for you, read each of the following questions and answer "Yes" or "No."

Yes	No	1.	*Are you personable and friendly?*
Yes	No	2.	*Can you speak clearly?*
Yes	No	3.	*Can you maintain a professional attitude in difficult circumstances?*
Yes	No	4.	*Would you be comfortable using firearms, self-defense techniques, and security equipment?*
Yes	No	5.	*Are you physically fit and can you stand and walk for lengthy periods?*
Yes	No	6.	*Would you be able to physically subdue someone if needed?*
Yes	No	7.	*Can you communicate information and ideas well?*
Yes	No	8.	*Do you think you can deal with emotionally* **overwrought** *and unstable people?*
Yes	No	9.	*Are you good at observing details and remembering information?*
Yes	No	10.	*Are you honest?*

If you answered "Yes" to most of these questions, you might consider a career as a court bailiff. To find out more about this job, read on.

What's the Work Like?

Court bailiffs provide security in the courtroom before and during court sessions. You are the law enforcement arm of the court. Your main job is to maintain order. Sometimes this means simply keeping people from talking while court is in session. Other times you will have to calm, restrain, or even physically remove disruptive individuals from the courtroom. In extreme cases, you may have to arrest unruly people. Some bailiffs are armed and in uniform.

TALKING MONEY

Salaries for court bailiffs vary a great deal, ranging between $23,000 and $74,000 a year, according to 2016 data from the U.S. Bureau of Labor Statistics. State employees tend to make more, while employees of local governments tend to make less. Median annual earnings are $42,670 a year. Bailiffs also receive excellent medical and retirement benefits.

Another important responsibility of the bailiff is to make sure no weapons or forbidden electronic or photographic equipment enters the courtroom. You will learn to operate security equipment such as **magnetometers**, handheld screening devices, and package X-ray machines. The bailiff also prevents people from entering the courtroom who are not properly dressed or behaved. You may also have to search the courtroom for smuggled goods.

A court bailiff also has the responsibility of taking care of the jury. Sometimes trials last for more than one day. On some of these occasions, judges decide that jurors cannot return to their homes until trials are over. In these situations, jurors must stay at hotels. Bailiffs guard

▲ A court bailiff uses an X-ray machine to inspect the contents of a woman's bag before allowing her to enter the courthouse.

these hotels and escort jurors to restaurants to keep the public from contacting them. Because of the bailiff's role in this situation, he or she is sometimes called the "jury shepherd." Once the jury is chosen, the bailiff is the only person who can communicate with them.

There is also a basic maintenance component to a court bailiff's job. You will have to inspect the courtroom for cleanliness and make sure all equipment is in good working order. You will also have to check the bench (the area where the judge sits) to make sure that the judge has adequate supplies, proper forms, and other materials. You'll also be responsible for the proper handling of all evidence and exhibits.

TALKING TRENDS

The crime level affects the number of jobs for court bailiffs. If the crime level increases, more bailiffs may be needed to control more offenders. The number of bailiffs may rise in the next few years as the quantity of lawsuits continues to grow. In addition, fear of terrorism has resulted in extra security at U.S. courts.

Who's Hiring?

- State court systems

- Local government court systems

- Private repossession agencies

Where Are the Jobs?

Court bailiffs obviously work in courts, so most jobs are located in urban areas. Even in rural areas, you will usually be working in the county seat, which is typically a larger city in the county. In a court bailiff position, most of your duties involve standing silently in the courtroom and patrolling the courthouse.

However, you are also responsible for transporting and supervising the movement of prisoners to and from court. That means you will guard criminal defendants accused of both misdemeanors and felonies and secure them in holding cells. It's your job if prisoners need to be transferred to other jails or institutions.

You may also get out of the courtroom when you escort, guard, and deliver material to sequestered juries. However, in general, the courtroom will be your home away from home.

A Typical Day

Here are the highlights of a typical day for a court bailiff.

Maintain order in the courtroom. It is your responsibility to enforce the rules of behavior in the courtroom. You'll warn people not to smoke or disturb court procedure. You'll also collect unauthorized weapons from people entering the courtroom.

Transport prisoners to and from the court. You have to make sure the prisoners are secure in holding cells. You might have to drive a prisoner from one jail to another.

▲ When emotions run high in a courtroom, it is a court bailiff's duty to maintain order. Here, a court bailiff separates angry family members outside the courtroom after a verdict was read in a very emotional trial.

NOTES FROM THE FIELD

Chief court constable, *Bowling Green, Ohio*

Q: *How did you get your job?*

A: I [was] employed with the Ohio State Patrol for eight years [and] General Motors . . . for 16 years. I was hired at Wood County [Ohio] Common Pleas Court to [work in the] security department for the courthouse complex. The duties of criminal bailiff and court constable are very similar.

Q: *What do you like best about your job?*

A: One of the things I like best about my job is that every day is different. The day goes by fast and I get involved with a lot of different projects and meetings, attend training conferences, and instruct new employees. I believe if you enjoy your job that is a major factor.

Q: *What is the most challenging part of your job?*

A: I work with employees, elected officials, the public, and my staff. Our courthouse complex has many different offices besides the courts. I need to make sure each day all the job positions are filled [and that] the main entrance, which is supplied with X-ray and metal detectors, is working correctly.

Q: *What are the keys to success to being a constable/bailiff?*

A: I enjoy keeping busy with challenging and different duties. I believe you should be dedicated to your job. You should also treat people like you would like to be treated, and use common sense and good judgment. If you do these things, your fellow workers and other people will respect you. I always try to do the best I can on any job assignment and return calls and requests in a timely manner. I take pride in my job and the work that I do. I try to be fair and honest with everyone.

"Shepherd" a jury. You will escort the jury to a restaurant or other areas outside the courtroom to prevent any jury contact with the public. If the jury is sequestered, you'll guard the locations where they stay.

Start Preparing Now

- Most bailiffs' positions require a high school diploma or a credential of general educational development (GED). English, social studies, and computing classes would probably be most beneficial.

- Sharpen up your clerical skills. Employers of bailiffs prefer people who know general office practices and can use computer systems. Bailiffs sometimes help execute and enforce a variety of court orders.

Training and How to Get It

All court bailiffs work for the government, whether federal, state, or local. Your employer will provide all the training you need to be a court bailiff. Many new employees learn their duties through on-the-job training. You will work with an experienced court bailiff as a mentor to learn the job. Because the job description varies widely from place to place, training is often site specific.

You will certainly be taught general knowledge of court procedures and legal terms. You will also have to learn various techniques in handling visitors to the court and in maintaining the behavior of prisoners. Because a bailiff is a peacekeeping position, you will be taught police procedures as well as the safe use and handling of firearms. In order to transport prisoners, you'll probably have to learn the geography of the county or local area in some depth.

Some court systems offer formal training programs. These programs usually take about one month to complete. You'll learn how to protect judges and defend yourself in close quarters. You'll also learn jury, prisoner, and evidence-handling procedures. Many training programs spend considerable time on the proper way to conduct searches and use security equipment.

Other skills you will need depend on your responsibilities. Some bailiffs have more clerical duties and will need to know how to complete and organize court documents, forms, and other records. Others will need skill in operating telecommunications systems. In larger court systems, general training is ongoing.

See a day in the life of a court bailiff.

▲ After being found guilty, a man is fingerprinted by the court bailiff before being transported to prison.

Learn the Lingo

Here are a few words you'll hear as a bailiff:

- **Cop a plea** Slang for a "plea bargain" in which an accused defendant agrees to plead guilty to a crime in return for a promise of leniency in sentencing.

- **Hung jury** A hopelessly deadlocked jury in a criminal case. Usually it means there is no unanimous verdict.

- **Priors** Slang for a criminal defendant's previous record of criminal charges or convictions.

- **TRO** This is short for a "temporary restraining order." A TRO is a court order to keep conditions exactly as they are until a court hearing can be held at which both sides will argue their case.

Finding a Job

The basic requirement for most court bailiffs' positions is any combination of education and experience equivalent to graduation from high school. You'll also need a valid driver's license. In most cases, you'll have to pass a background check and a drug-screening test. Senior officers will then interview you to determine your judgment, integrity, and sense of responsibility. Some agencies have psychologists perform the interviews or administer personality tests. Bailiffs usually must be 21 or older.

Employers look for applicants who have good communication skills. Some employers prefer applicants who have a background in law enforcement. Knowledge of weaponry, public safety, and security operations is also helpful.

In some cases, the local sheriff's office provides deputy sheriffs to fill the role of court bailiff. In some states, the court officers are sworn peace officers and are employed by an office of court administration. In other places, a bailiff's position is a civil service position based on an exam. The test usually measures your knowledge of legal and criminal procedures, clerical skills, and problem-solving ability. Applicants are chosen based on their test score and other criteria.

LEARN MORE ONLINE

NEW YORK STATE SUPREME COURT OFFICER'S ASSOCIATION
This Web site has news articles and includes some useful New York–centric links. http://www.nysscoa.org

INSTITUTE FOR COURT SECURITY
Part of the National Sheriff's Association, the Institute for Court Security provides educational materials and training programs for bailiffs and other court officers. https://www.sheriffs.org/global-center-for-public-safety/institute-court-security

Tips for Success

- Maintain mental alertness. A bailiff's position often consists of a great deal of routine work mixed with a few rare moments of high drama. A crucial skill is the ability to analyze situations quickly and adopt an effective and reasonable course of action under pressure.

- Keep up with court rules and regulations. Your job is to maintain order and uphold the rules of the courtroom. Make sure you are up-to-date with the latest procedures, protocols, and other matters related to the execution of your responsibilities.

▲ A court officer stands guard outside a courtroom.

Reality Check

Although courtroom work has moments of high drama and excitement, much of the day is routine. Be prepared for stretches of relatively mundane clerical duties.

Related Jobs to Consider

Police officer. Working as a police officer is more rewarding than being a bailiff. However, the job is more stressful, the hours are worse, and the risks are much greater.

Correctional officer. As a correctional officer, you can continue to provide security in the criminal justice system.

Paralegal. This job keeps you involved in the legal environment without any security concerns or fears.

How to Move Up

- Pursue a career in law enforcement. Bailiffs can join the sheriff's department or the police department. It's a good stepping-stone to more active law enforcement positions.

- Move into a supervisory position. Bailiffs with leadership skills may want to advance to supervise the other bailiffs on their shift. You may need more training to advance to higher positions.

TEXT-DEPENDENT QUESTIONS

1. *What are some of the tasks that court bailiffs perform?*

2. *Why are bailiffs sometimes called "jury shepherds"?*

3. *What is a hung jury?*

4. *What are some tips for success in this field?*

RESEARCH PROJECTS

1. *If you are old enough, seek out a summer or part-time job in the security field. Even a position in a mall will show that you are serious about law enforcement as a career.*

2. *Find out more about what goes on in a courtroom. Courthouses are public buildings, and it's likely you can visit or even tour one in your community. If not, start with articles like "In the Courtroom: Who Does What?" (http://litigation.findlaw.com/going-to-court/in-the-courtroom-who-does-what.html) and "How Courts Work" (https://www.americanbar.org/groups/public_education/resources/law_related_education_network/how_courts_work/cc_trials.html).*

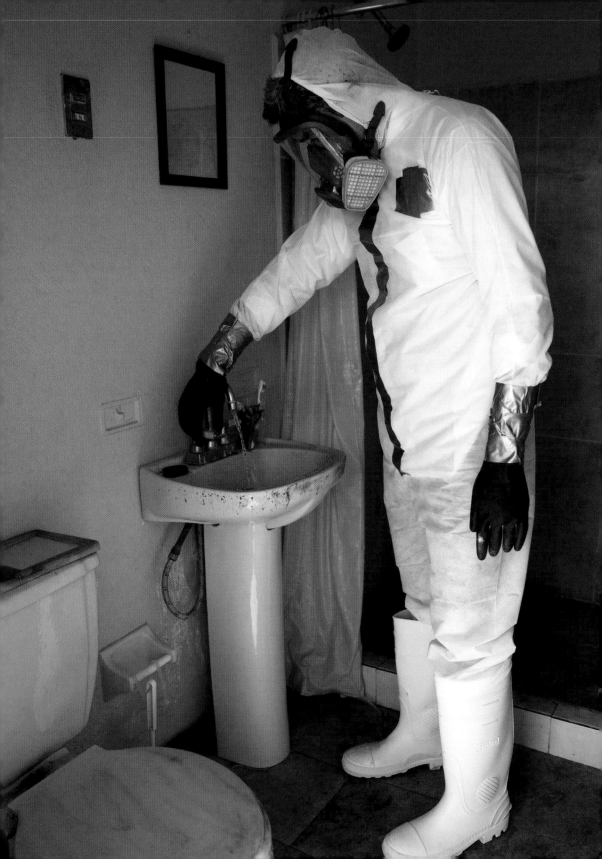

Crime-Scene Cleaner

3

Assist after police complete investigation. Help people avoid emotional stress. Perform essential public health work.

WORDS TO UNDERSTAND

coroner: an official who investigates causes of death.

detoxification: the process of removing poisonous or dangerous substances.

pathogens: microorganisms that can cause disease.

squeamish: describes someone who is easily upset or nauseated by things like blood.

When the police and firefighters arrive at the scene of a violent death, they do not usually clean up the mess. That is the responsibility of the property owner or the occupant. However, most family members, and even cleaning companies, want no part of cleaning a wall splattered with blood. This is where crime-scene cleaners come in. Crime-scene cleaners clean, disinfect, and restore the crime-scene site to its previous state.

This is not a job for **squeamish** people. Crime-scene cleaners deal with bodily fluids, bone fragments, dangerous substances, and explosive chemicals—not to mention grieving relatives. Nonetheless, cleaning a crime scene is an essential public health job. As a crime-scene cleaner, you spare family and friends the emotional trauma of having to clean up a home

◀ **A crime-scene cleaner gets to work cleaning a bathroom after homicide investigators have left. The cleaner will remove any bodily fluids or chemical residue left behind.**

or business after the death or severe injury of a loved one or employee. At the same time, you can earn a good salary for this essential work.

Is This the Right Job for You?

To find out if being a crime-scene cleaner is a good fit for you, read each of the following questions and answer "Yes" or "No."

Yes	No	**1.**	*Can you handle the sight of blood and guts?*
Yes	No	**2.**	*Can you maintain a good attitude dealing with a scene of a death?*
Yes	No	**3.**	*Do you act professionally under difficult circumstances?*
Yes	No	**4.**	*Are you dependable and detail oriented?*
Yes	No	**5.**	*Do you have good stamina?*
Yes	No	**6.**	*Can you handle working for long hours in a biohazard suit?*
Yes	No	**7.**	*Do you follow directions extremely well?*
Yes	No	**8.**	*Would you be comfortable working with dangerous substances?*
Yes	No	**9.**	*Can you manage being on call 24/7?*
Yes	No	**10.**	*Are you sensitive to the needs of other people?*

If you answered "Yes" to most of these questions, you might consider a career as a crime-scene cleaner. To find out more about this job, read on.

What's the Work Like?

As a crime-scene cleaner, you usually arrive after the police, firefighters, and **coroner**. The most common cleanup situations include the scene of a violent death, the discovery of a decomposing body, or a site of illicit operations, such as an illegal methamphetamine lab that has been busted by the police. In all cases, your job is to remove any sign of the crime incident. More importantly, you must make sure no hazardous substances, such as blood or dangerous chemicals, remain at the site.

In the case of murders, suicides, or accidental deaths, you have to deal with bodily fluids carrying bacteria and maybe even infectious agents, such as HIV. You use powerful disinfectants to wipe or scrub every drop of blood off of all surfaces, including floors, counters, ceilings, walls, lights, artwork, and appliances. You rip out and discard any blood-soaked carpeting, upholstery, or rugs. Sometimes this requires hours of scrubbing in a plastic suit. The coroner usually removes a decomposing body before any cleanup starts. However, you still have to clean up the leftover body matter and take care of the smell.

A methamphetamine (meth) lab isn't as sickening as a death scene, but it's often more dangerous to clean up. The chemicals used to make methamphetamine, a popular illegal street drug, leave a poisonous trace that coats every surface and stays in the air. At a meth lab site, you have to destroy everything that could not be dipped in **detoxification** chemicals. All furniture, cabinets, light fixtures, and carpets would have to be disposed of. In some cases, you demolish virtually the entire building in order to clean the site.

TALKING MONEY

The U.S. Bureau of Labor Statistics does not list crime-scene cleaner as a job category, but if we think of it as a type of hazardous materials removal, we can get a general sense of the pay scale. Workers in that field earn an average of $19.54 per hour or $40,640 per year. Overtime is very common, which can increase earnings. Wages also vary a lot depending on location; it's even possible to reach six figures in a large city.

As a crime-scene cleaner, you may also be called to clean up a contaminated chemical spill at a factory, an anthrax exposure site, or the scene of a terrorist attack.

▲ Crime-scene cleaners need to be extremely careful when entering an illegal methamphetamine "meth" lab. Hazmat suits must be worn to clean up any remaining chemical residue.

Who's Hiring?

- Specialized crime-scene cleanup companies

- Cleaning companies that occasionally do crime scenes

- Hazardous-materials-removal companies

- Self-employed

TALKING TRENDS

Crime, violence, and death will always be with us. That means there's no end of work for crime-scene cleaners. Salaries and job opportunities are expected to rise as governments increasingly shift this work to private companies.

Where Are the Jobs?

As a crime-scene cleaner, you will almost certainly work for a private employer. The personalities and rules of the company will go a long way in determining your job satisfaction. Companies vary widely over pay, benefits, work rules, work hours, and the like. Once you break into the business, it's essential to find a company that suits your needs.

The location of your work will depend on the incident. Homicides and suicides can take place anywhere, whether on an old farm, in a suburban ranch house, or in an apartment in

▲ Men clean up debris after a terror-related explosion.

the inner city. Most crime scenes are indoors; accidents and homicides can certainly occur outdoors, but there's less to clean up.

Frequently, crime-scene cleaners must complete their work in the presence of the victim's family or friends. This means workers must be able to deal with the immediate anger or sadness of those in mourning. People who loved the victim may be watching while the cleaners are scrubbing blood off the walls. They may be hysterical and looking for support. Crime-scene cleaners must remain detached enough to handle disgusting physical remains and yet stay sensitive to a family's tragedy. It's a difficult balancing act.

Crime-scene cleaners work regular hours, such as a 9-to-5 or 8-to-4 shift. However, crimes don't happen only during the day, and you have to be on call regularly. In addition, there's no way to predict how long the next job may take. Cleaning up the scene of a messy homicide, suicide, or undiscovered death can take anywhere from a couple of hours to three 16-hour days.

A Typical Day

Here are the highlights for a typical day for a crime-scene cleaner.

Assess the scene and the damage. When the cleaners arrive, they decide what to do to return the room, apartment, or house to its preincident state.

▲ A hazardous material removal team assesses the job after a car containing swimming pool chemicals tipped over. The team must wear hazmat suits and carefully clean up poisonous liquids so that they are not released into the environment.

NOTES FROM THE FIELD

Crime-scene cleaner, Woolley, Washington

Q: *How did you get your job?*

A: I got the idea of cleaning crime scenes while working as a carpet cleaner. I was sent to a house to extract some blood from a mattress and some carpeting, and it got me thinking: "Who cleans up the messes when someone is murdered, commits suicide, or even passes away naturally?" So I started asking around. I called the coroner's office first, and he said that there were people who did this exact thing for a living. He also told me that there was a demand for the service in my area.

I went to OSHA [Occupational Safety and Health Administration] and asked what I needed to do legally to perform this business. At the time there was no special licensing or permits necessary because crime-scene cleaning was only viewed as a form of janitorial work. But I was told there were certain procedures in how to dispose of biohazard waste. So I learned those and followed them. All that was left was learning about chemicals and buying equipment.

Q: *What do you like best about your job?*

A: The best part of the job, I am sorry to say, is the money. It provides a great relief and service to a family in need during their grieving process, but it also pays a lot of money. Typically, one can make $2,000 to $10,000 in one day's work.

Q: *What's the most challenging part of your job?*

A: Safety is of the utmost concern. Airborne pathogens are nothing to play around with. Hepatitis C is one disease that some victims have had that I successfully prevented myself from getting.

A typical day starts with a lot of safety gear. Respirators are a must. When you first go into the house you enter with sprayer in hand—spraying disinfectant in front of you on the floor as you go. Next you remove and clean all furniture that may have been infected or sprayed by bodily fluids. In some cases (depending on the client's wishes), I go in and clean everything. In other cases, I go in and remove and throw away everything. Sometimes, I have had to scrape acoustical ceiling paint off in a room. The tool I probably use the most in cleaning is just a shop vac. The very worst part of crime-scene cleaning is the smell. You never get used to the smell of death.

Q: *What are the keys to success to being a crime-scene cleaner?*

A: Learn the laws; learn about cleaning bio waste; learn about disposing of bio waste; and learn about your own safety. There are a lot of diseases out there, and not all of them die along with the victim.

Clean up the site. This may mean putting on personal protective gear, such as a suit, gloves, filtered respirators, and chemical-spill boots. A lot of the job is simply hard scrubbing with mops, buckets, spray bottles, sponges, and brushes. Dangerous or contaminated substances are placed in 55-gallon, hard-plastic biohazard-waste containers

See what it's like to clean up a crime scene.

Dispose of the evidence. You can't put hazardous waste in a regular trash dump. Crime-scene cleaners need a special government permit to transport it. Blood and gore has to be burned in a medical-waste incinerator. Poisonous chemical waste can only be dumped in special areas far away from the public. You have to transport the waste wherever it needs to go.

Start Preparing Now

- Take science courses. A little chemistry can be extremely useful when determining which chemicals remove certain substances and how chemicals react to one another. Biology is also useful for knowing your way around human body parts.

- Be familiar with construction work. A construction background is helpful because some cleanup sites, such as meth labs, require that walls and built-in structures be removed.

Training and How to Get It

You don't need any official degree to be a crime-scene cleaner. As of 2017, there was minimal government regulation of the crime-scene cleaning industry. That's both good and bad.

It means that you can be a crime-scene cleaner, but it also means just about anyone can be a crime-scene cleaner.

OSHA does have some regulations that pertain to crime-scene cleanups. For example, OSHA forbids anyone from working with blood or body fluids if they haven't had "blood-borne pathogen" training. Your employer is required to give you that training. In addition, government permits are required to transport and dispose of the dangerous waste.

Most crime-scene cleaning companies require their employees to take certification courses. These may include classes on the dangers, characteristics, and appropriate safety procedures for handling bodily fluids. You should also receive training on the proper use of protective gear in addition to learning how to correctly transport and dispose of dangerous waste.

Some crime-scene cleanup companies require workers to pass a "gross" test to make sure they can handle the work without throwing up. This type of training may be a realistic visual presentation of photos from previous cleanups to an actual cleanup of animal remains.

Crime-scene cleaners also need to keep up-to-date on vaccinations and stay informed about how to protect themselves against infectious diseases found in blood and other substances. It's essential to have a hepatitis B vaccine every five years. Of course, it is essential to be in good overall health and physical condition.

Learn the Lingo

Here are a few words you'll hear as a crime-scene cleaner:

- **CTS decon** This stands for "crime and trauma scene decontamination." CTS decon is the official industry name for crime-scene cleanup, particularly when it involves cleaning up dangerous materials.

- **Hazmat suit** A full-body suit worn as protection from hazardous substances. Hazmat suits usually include breathing air supplies to provide uncontaminated air for the user. Working in a hazmat suit is very tiring.

- **Garbage house** A garbage house is a house or apartment, usually rented, that the occupants have turned into a veritable trash dump and sometimes a giant toilet. Crime-scene cleaners are often called to get these back up to code.

Finding a Job

There is a lot of turnover in the crime-scene cleaning business: it's an exhausting job, and most people burn out quickly. On the other hand, that means job opportunities are plentiful. Many potential workers don't want the job because they prefer cleanup work that is less stressful and less dangerous. Oftentimes, people who go into crime-scene cleanup have previously worked in other health, safety, or medical jobs. They have seen blood and gore and know what to expect.

To find a job, simply contact a company that you think you'd like to work for. You can find these relatively easily on the Internet and less frequently in a phone book. (Try under "Cleaning" and "Housecleaning.") Crime-scene cleanup companies are usually located in large cities where there's enough work to make them profitable. You don't need any experience; the company will train you. It helps to have a work record of dependability and responsibility. You must be available to work irregular hours. If a job isn't open, be persistent. Crime-scene cleaning has an unusually high turnover rate; a job that didn't exist today may be there tomorrow.

Tips for Success

- Have a strong stomach. You'll run into some pretty gruesome and scary stuff at this job. You need the ability to emotionally detach yourself from your work.

- Be accustomed to cleaning. Any regular cleaning job can prepare you for work in this field.

▲ A crime-scene cleaner removes blood from a bedroom floor at a murder scene.

Reality Check

The money's good but you could be spending eight hours a day in a plastic suit moving furniture and scrubbing floors. Don't forget you'll also be on call 24 hours a day. Are you ready for it?

Related Jobs to Consider

Hazardous-materials removal worker. These workers perform similar jobs but without the blood and gore. They are often involved in asbestos or lead removal.

Building cleaning worker. There are more than 4 million building-cleaning workers in the United States. They work in nearly every type of establishment. It doesn't pay as well but there's much less stress.

Emergency medical technician (EMT). EMTs perform prehospital medical procedures in incidents as varied as automobile accidents, heart attacks, drownings, childbirth, and gunshot wounds.

LEARN MORE ONLINE

AMDECON

This is the Web site of a company specializing in suicide, homicide, human decomposition, and meth lab cleanup. http://www.amdecon.com

CRIME AND TRAUMA SCENE DECONTAMINATION TRAINING ACADEMY

This is an example of an online and hands-on training program for people interested in a career in this field. http://www.cts-decon-training-academy.com

How to Move Up

- Become your own boss. Your best chance of having a satisfying career in this field is owning your own crime-scene cleaning business. Self-employed CTS decon people charge between $100 and $600 an hour. You need good contacts with the mortuaries, funeral homes, homicide departments, and district attorney's office in your area.

- Take some classes. Working with dead bodies can be exhausting. If you take a few classes at a local community college, you can switch to being an EMT. It's a different kind of stress.

- Train or teach others. The field is growing, and there's a need for people who can train cleaners. Who better than someone with experience actually doing it?

TEXT-DEPENDENT QUESTIONS

1. What types of hazardous materials do crime scene cleaners encounter?

2. What is a typical day like?

3. What training is required?

4. What are some alternative jobs you might consider?

RESEARCH PROJECTS

1. Although there is no specific government regulation for crime scene cleanup companies, there are quite a few different certifications that cleaners may need. Search online for a list of hazardous materials certifications (you can get started here: https://www.biorecovery.com/about-crime-scene-cleaners/certifications/), and then find out what is required to get those certifications. The more you have, the more valuable an employee you'll be.

2. Find out what this job is really like by reading some journalistic accounts, such as "Smelling Death" by Saira Khan (https://www.theatlantic.com/business/archive/2014/07/the-smell-of-death-a-day-on-the-job-with-new-yorks-crime-scene-cleaners/374022/) and "The Daily Life of a Crime Scene Cleaner" by Jennifer Welsh (http://www.businessinsider.com/the-daily-life-of-a-crime-scene-cleaner-2013-7).

Security Guard

Protect lives and property. Act independently.
Work flexible hours.

WORDS TO UNDERSTAND

CPR: short for cardiopulmonary resuscitation, a life-saving technique to restart the heart and get oxygen to the brain.

deter: discourage or scare off.

gaming surveillance officer: a type of security guard who works at casinos.

Security guard positions come in all shapes and sizes. In general, guards protect their employer's property and maintain the security of the establishment. In some cases, they also protect people. Security guards usually wear uniforms and protect property simply by being extremely visible. They also watch, either through patrolling or by looking at alarm systems, for signs of crime, fire, or disorder. They report any suspicious incidents to their employer and call for whatever emergency services are necessary.

Concern about crime, vandalism, and terrorism continues to increase the need for security guards. However, it is important to remember that security guards, even if they wear badges or uniforms, are not police officers. A security guard who claims to be a police officer is committing

◀ **A security guard keeps an eye out for any suspicious or inappropriate behavior during a sporting event.**

a crime (as is any person who is not a police officer). Yet security guards, like police officers, often put themselves in harm's way to protect property, the public, or fellow employees.

Is This the Right Job for You?

To find out if being a security guard is a good fit for you, read each of the following questions and answer "Yes" or "No."

Yes	No	1. *Do you consider yourself dependable, reliable, and responsible?*
Yes	No	2. *Can you work irregular hours while managing your sleep needs?*
Yes	No	3. *Can you maintain a professional attitude in difficult circumstances?*
Yes	No	4. *Do you have keen observation skills?*
Yes	No	5. *Are you physically fit and do you have quick reflexes?*
Yes	No	6. *Can you work independently without direct supervision?*
Yes	No	7. *Can you handle a job with an element of danger?*
Yes	No	8. *Can you maintain concentration despite a lack of constant stimulation?*
Yes	No	9. *Are you prompt?*
Yes	No	10. *Can you keep your cool even in difficult situations?*

If you answered "Yes" to most of these questions, consider a career as a security guard. To find out more about this job, read on.

What's the Work Like?

As a security guard, you patrol and inspect property to protect against terrorism, fire, theft, and vandalism. The security officer's motto is "Detect, **deter**, observe, and report." It's not generally your job to detain people you suspect of committing crimes, especially given that most security guards do not carry weapons. No matter how much training you have, you probably don't have as much experience

TALKING MONEY

The average security guard salary in 2016 was $25,840 per year, according to data from the U.S. Bureau of Labor Statistics. Gaming surveillance officers are paid more, earning an average of $35,420. Outside of casinos, the best-paying jobs are usually in state government, at sites that require high security.

as—and you definitely do not have the authority of—experienced police officers. It's not worth getting killed for the sake of your employer's property.

Your job responsibilities vary depending on the size, type, and location of your employer. They also vary depending on whether you work in a single, set security position or on a mobile patrol. You may be stationed at a guard desk inside a building. In that case, you do not patrol. Instead, you watch electronic security devices or check the identification of people entering or leaving the building. You may also be assigned to a guardhouse outside the entrance to a gated facility or community. Your job here is to make sure that employees and visitors display proper identification before entering. You may have a portable radio or cell phone to keep in regular contact with a central station.

On the other hand, guards assigned to mobile patrol duty drive or walk from location to location. This may involve working indoors or outdoors in any kind of weather. You must

▲ A guard monitors multiple security cameras during his shift.

conduct security checks in a specific assigned area. If needed, you call for assistance from police, fire, or emergency medical services.

Security guards usually work eight-hour shifts and 40-hour weeks. Some employers have three shifts, and guards rotate to divide daytime, weekend, and holiday work equally.

TALKING TRENDS

The fear of terrorism has driven the increased need for security guards, and the Bureau of Labor Statistics reports that hiring is expected to grow. However, there is stiff competition for higher-paying positions at facilities requiring longer periods of training, such as nuclear power plants and weapons installations.

Who's Hiring?

- Investigation and security services, including guard and armored car services. (More than half of all jobs for security guards are in these fields. These organizations provide security on a contract basis. They assign their guards to sites as they are needed.)

- Schools, hospitals, malls, theme parks, restaurants, bars, hotels, department stores, construction sites, apartment houses, casinos, manufacturing firms, and owners of real estate.

- City, state, and federal government.

- Private patrol companies that protect several client sites.

Where Are the Jobs?

In 2016 there were well over a million security guards, working at a huge variety of different locations. Security guards in department stores and malls protect people, money, and merchandise. They often work with undercover store detectives to prevent theft by customers or employees. Some shopping centers and theaters have security officers who patrol their parking lots to prevent car thefts and robberies.

Security guards in banks, hospitals, and office buildings ensure the safety of the institutions' workers, property, and customers. At air, sea, and rail terminals, guards protect people, freight, and equipment. They may prevent terrorism by screening passengers and visitors for

NOTES FROM THE FIELD

Security guard, West Mifflin, Pennsylvania

Q: How did you get your job?

A: I started working with Allied Barton Securities about a year ago. I needed to get some experience [in the workforce]. I thought this would be the key.

Q: What do you like best about your job?

A: For me, the best part of my job is dealing with people night after night.

Q: What's the most challenging part of your job?

A: Well, it really depends. Working the night shift on certain days, you'll have your fair share of fire drills, nutcases, or whatnot. It really keeps me on my feet at times.

Q: What are the keys to success to being a security guard?

A: I think the best advice I could give a person who wants to get into security is just be the type of person who shows up for work. A major issue my company has at my site has been firing people left and right for absenteeism.

weapons and explosives. Or they might simply watch for fires and make sure that nothing is stolen while a vehicle is being loaded or unloaded.

Guards who work in public buildings, such as museums or art galleries, protect exhibits by inspecting people and packages entering and leaving the building. Guards working at universities, parks, and sports stadiums control crowd movement, supervise parking and seating, and direct traffic.

Many security positions have been created after the terrorist attacks on the United States in 2001. In factories, laboratories, government buildings, data processing centers, and military bases, security officers protect information, products, computer codes, and defense secrets.

The list could go on and on. The examples above only brush the surface of possible working environments for security guards.

▲ A security guard stands in front of a painting at a museum. His job is to make sure museum visitors do not get too close or touch the artwork.

A Typical Day

Here are some highlights for a typical shift as a security guard.

Observe and report. Regular patrol is usually part of a security guard's duties. The work is routine, but you must be alert for threats to you and the property you are protecting. You may well have to deal with at least one minor emergency, such as a lost person, lockout, or dead vehicle battery.

Deal with the public. Guards who work during the day may have a great deal of contact with other employees and members of the public.

Fill out forms. No matter where you work, you will have to take accurate notes and write effective reports. Firms want a written record of what occurred during your shift, such as violations or suspicious behavior. You may also have to interview witnesses or victims and prepare case reports.

▲ Security teams are often needed for large crowds. They may be called in to supervise music festivals, sporting events, and the like.

Start Preparing Now

- Get a driver's license. This is a prerequisite for many security jobs.

- Take first aid classes. Security guards, like all public safety workers, benefit from a basic knowledge of first aid and **CPR**. It also makes getting a job easier.

- Learn to use firearms. Guards who have training and certification for firearms can usually get a higher-paying job with more responsibility (and of course, more risks).

Training and How to Get It

Many employers of unarmed guards do not have any educational requirements at all. However, employers who want armed guards will likely require that applicants have the equivalent of a high school diploma and some work experience.

The amount of training guards receive varies. Many employers give newly hired guards instruction before they start the job and provide on-the-job training. Security guards may learn public relations, report writing, crisis deterrence, and first aid, as well as any specialized training that relates to their particular assignment. They may also be trained on topics such as sharing information with law enforcement, preventing crime, handling evidence, properly using force, testifying in court, writing a report, communication skills, and emergency-response procedures.

Many states require a license to work as a security guard. However, the training requirements for a license are usually minimal. A licensed security guard usually must be at least 18 years old and pass background, criminal record, and fingerprint checks. There may also be a requirement for classroom training in subjects such as property rights, emergency procedures, and the detention of suspected criminals. Many employers also require random drug testing that may continue as long as you have the job.

Armed security guards protect sensitive sites, such as military installations, banks, dams, and nuclear power plants. Training requirements are higher for armed guards because their employers are legally responsible for any use of force. Armed guards need additional permits and receive formal training for carrying weapons, such as batons, firearms, and pepper spray. Armed guard positions have much stricter background checks and entry requirements than those of unarmed guards. Security guards who carry firearms may be periodically tested in their use.

Learn the Lingo

Here are a few words to know as a security guard:

- **Backup** An additional assisting security guard.

- **Guard tour patrol system** A way of making sure a security guard actually patrols when and where he or she is assigned to patrol. The system is now usually electronic.

- **OC, or OC spray** A chemical agent used to subdue a combative person. It's named after its main ingredient, oleoresin capsicum, which is also the active ingredient in hot peppers.

Learn what it takes to become a security guard.

- **Turkey bacon** Derogatory name for a private security guard; similar to "rent-a-cop." Used by security guards in both a positive and negative way.

Finding a Job

In 2016, there were more than 1 million security guards employed in the United States. You can find these positions advertised in help-wanted ads in newspapers, as well as on Web sites such as USA Jobs, CareerBuilder, US Job Bank, and Monster. Security guard positions are available at most employment agencies. Some openings are civil service positions and will be posted at the state employment office. They're even easy to get by walking Main Street or the mall, filling out job applications. The turnover rate of security guards is very high, so it's vital that you don't forget your phone number on your résumé—an employer may want to hire you on short notice.

Applicants for a security guard position should have good character references and no serious police record. They should be emotionally stable, mentally alert, and physically fit to cope with the job requirements. Guards who frequently have contact with the public should possess good communication skills.

LEARN MORE ONLINE

AMERICAN SOCIETY FOR INDUSTRIAL SECURITY
With 35,000 members, this is the largest international organization for security professionals. This Web site has a wide range of interesting information on a career in security, including a help-wanted section. http://www.asisonline.org

UNITED GOVERNMENT SECURITY OFFICERS OF AMERICA
This union, founded in 1992, represents security officers on federal contracts. http://www.ugsoa.com

SECURITY POLICE AND FIRE PROFESSIONALS OF AMERICA
The Web site of this association, which has represented security guards since the 1950s, features a job bank. http://www.spfpa.org

Tips for Success

- Maintain good judgment and common sense. All security officers need to have a professional attitude. They have to be able to take charge and direct others in emergencies or other dangerous incidents.

- Stay fit. Guards go through stretches of inactivity and can get out of shape if they are not careful. It's important to keep your body in condition.

Reality Check

The job is repetitive and boring 99 percent of the time. During the other 1 percent of the time, many security guards are exposed to serious risks. It takes a particular kind of person to deal with this combination of inactivity and intense activity.

▲ A security guard takes the night shift as he sits in his booth at an entry gate.

Related Jobs to Consider

Correctional officer. A form of security work, only guarding criminals instead of property. The pay and benefits are usually better than security guard work, but the hassles can be greater.

Police officer. This is a related security and protective service. Like guards, the police protect property, maintain security, and enforce regulations. In fact, many police officers work a second job as security guards.

Private investigator. This is a more challenging job than security guard work but one that draws similarly on powers of observation and a tolerance for long quiet periods. Private investigators use many methods to determine the facts in a variety of matters. Specialized training is usually required.

How to Move Up

• Advance within your organization. Many people do not stay long as security guards. This means opportunities for advancement are good for career security officers. With a little experience and training, you can move up to a supervisor or security manager position.

- Move outside your organization. Salaries differ tremendously depending on the security level of the establishment. You can sometimes gain a higher-paying job with a different organization.

- Open your own agency. If you have management skills and ambition, you can try to open your own contract security guard agency.

- Switch to a law enforcement career. Many security officers, especially young people, use a security guard job as a way to get into a police career.

TEXT-DEPENDENT QUESTIONS

1. *What are some types of environments where security guards work?*

2. *What kind of training is required?*

3. *What is a guard tour patrol system?*

4. *How can you move up in this field?*

RESEARCH PROJECTS

1. *As mentioned above, having a basic knowledge of first aid may make you more attractive to employers. Get started now by taking a first-aid course, such as those offered by the Red Cross (http://www.redcross.org/m/phssmrd/take-a-class). Your school, local community college, or firehouse might also offer classes.*

2. *Find out how to get trained as a security guard: search online for "security guard training" and your area. You might also check out Security Guard Training Central (https://www.securityguardtrainingcentral.com/), which has lots of information about training for different types of security positions.*

Correctional Officer

Ensure the security of prisons. Provide inmates with needed programs and services. Be a positive role model.

5

WORDS TO UNDERSTAND

bailiffs: officials of the court who look after prisoners.

incarcerated: held in prison or jail.

penal: relating to the punishment of offenders.

proximity: closeness in space or time.

The United States has more people in prisons and jails than any other country in the world. As of 2017, more than 2.3 million people were behind bars. According to the Prison Policy Initiative, about 1.3 million were in state prisons, and 630,000 in local jails, and nearly 200,000 in federal prisons. These numbers have created a huge job market for correctional officers to watch over the people who are **incarcerated**. Correctional officers make sure that offenders serve their sentences of imprisonment in facilities that are safe, humane, and secure. This job puts you in close **proximity** with convicted criminals, which can be stressful, depressing, and potentially dangerous. But being a correctional officer can also be rewarding when you have a positive influence on the inmates you supervise.

◀ **A correctional officer escorts new prisoners off of a bus.**

Is This the Right Job for You?

To find out if being a correctional officer is a good fit for you, read each of the following questions and answer "Yes" or "No."

Yes	No	**1.** *Can you maintain a professional attitude in difficult circumstances?*
Yes	No	**2.** *Can you stand for four hours without a break?*
Yes	No	**3.** *Are you afraid of people with criminal backgrounds?*
Yes	No	**4.** *Do you get easily depressed?*
Yes	No	**5.** *Would you mind a job that required a great deal of routine work?*
Yes	No	**6.** *Are you conscientious about paperwork?*
Yes	No	**7.** *Can you keep your cool, even in difficult situations?*
Yes	No	**8.** *Do you consider yourself dependable, reliable, and responsible?*
Yes	No	**9.** *Do you have good communication skills?*
Yes	No	**10.** *Can you work under direct supervision?*

If you answered "Yes" to most of these questions, you might consider a career as a correctional officer. To find out more about this job, read on.

What's the Work Like?

A correctional officer is a person who guards and supervises inmates in a prison or jail. You will help maintain the security, discipline, and welfare of people who are waiting for a trial or who are serving time in a correctional facility. This means you will supervise prisoners during work, meals, recreation, bathing, and all other activities. You will also escort prisoners between the penal institution and courtrooms, medical facilities, and other destinations. Another crucial job is to make sure that inmates know, understand, and obey the rules and regulations of the institution.

The government depends on correctional officers to prevent disturbances, assaults, and escapes.

TALKING MONEY

Correctional officers earn an average about $42,820 a year. The top 10 percent earn more than $74,300 while the lowest 10 percent earn less than $23,300, according to 2017 data from the U.S. Bureau of Labor Statistics. In addition, correctional officers tend to receive excellent benefits.

▲ A guard stands watch on the wall at Washington State Reformatory.

You might have to guard a tower, gate, or fence. If someone escapes, you'll help search for and recapture him or her.

Being a correctional officer is a nosy business. You'll have to regularly count and search inmates and inspect their living quarters. You are also responsible for the safety and security of a correctional facility. You'll check cells for unhealthy conditions, smuggled goods, fire hazards, and any evidence of broken rules. In addition, you'll examine locks, window bars, doors, and gates to make sure that no one has tampered with them. Correctional officers also admit, instruct, and supervise authorized visitors to inmates.

There is also a written component to the job. You'll have to report in writing on inmate conduct, report security violations, disturbances, and any unusual occurrences. Officers often keep a daily log or record of their activities.

You will usually work unarmed if a jail or prison has direct supervision cell blocks, where the inmates are continually monitored. You'll have communication devices so that you can call for help if necessary. In high-security facilities, correctional officers often watch the activities of prisoners from a central control center using closed-circuit television cameras and a computer tracking system.

Who's Hiring?

- State and federal prisons

- Privately owned and managed prisons

- City and county jails or other penal institutions run by local governments

Where Are the Jobs?

Correctional officers work in different-sized **penal** institutions. Some

TALKING TRENDS

In 2016, there were more than 460,000 correctional officers in the United States, including jailers and **bailiffs**. Job opportunities for correctional officers are expected to decline in the next 10 years. Shrinking state budgets and changes in sentencing guidelines may limit the number of jobs being created. However, the need to replace correctional officers who leave or retire creates thousands of job openings each year.

work in very tightly controlled, maximum-security prisons. Others work in groups of low-security buildings that are more like college campuses than prisons. Some work in small, minimum-security conservation camps located in rural areas. A few correctional officers are

▲ A correctional officer monitors inmates during outdoor activities.

assigned to community correctional centers located in major cities. Other officers watch people held by the U.S. Citizenship and Immigration Services. A small number work for correctional institutions run by private, for-profit organizations.

Correctional officers work both indoors and outdoors. Conditions can vary widely. Some institutions are well lighted and air-conditioned but other facilities are run-down, overcrowded, and hot. Correctional officers usually work an eight-hour day and a five-day week. However, officers work all hours of the day and night, as well as on weekends and holidays. After all, prison and jail security must be provided around the clock. In many cases, correctional officers may be required to work paid overtime.

A Typical Day

Here are some aspects of a typical day as a correctional officer.

Patrol a cell block. You will probably work in a cell block alone or with another officer. Cell blocks usually house about 50 to 100 inmates. You will enforce regulations, through interpersonal communications skills and the use of punishments, such as the removal of privileges.

▲ A correctional officer pats down an incoming inmate, searching him for weapons and contraband before he enters the facility.

NOTES FROM THE FIELD

Correctional officer, Kingsley, Michigan

Q: *How did you get your job?*

A: I applied to be a corrections officer in Atlanta, Georgia, in 1990. For two years [I worked with] male prisoners, then they changed me over to female inmates. Requirements to be a correctional officer in the state of Georgia were military service or a college degree. I am a navy veteran.

Q: *What do you like best about your job?*

A: It feels great for me to be in uniform. Every day brings something new. Every correctional officer has several stories about events in the past. I like the conversations I have. The prisoners all want attention. I've learned and seen things and gone through quite a bit. I have surprised myself at how I was able to deal with some of the situations. We all have easy days, and some days we have are adrenaline-pumped-up situations. Every correctional officer develops relationships with other C.O.s and prisoners. I've also learned that TV [shows don't capture the reality of] being inside of a prison, with a few exceptions that really go into a prison and interview prisoners and C.O.s.

Q: *What is the most challenging part of your job?*

A: I do not advise this as a career unless you're sure of your choice. Some of the duty posts require that you stay locked up for your eight hours. Some require that you actually stand there and watch the prisoners shower.

There are three shifts to work on: 6 a.m. to 2 p.m., 2 p.m. to 10 p.m., and 10 p.m. to 6 a.m. So, a typical day is to meet in the briefing room, where the lieutenant briefs you on what happened on the previous shift, such as any troubled prisoners. Then everyone goes to their posts (medical, kitchen, housing unit, etc.). Once at your post, you begin the daily cleanup, supervision, and paperwork, specifically the logbooks. You check them for any discrepancies or problems on the post. You wake the prisoners, and they go to their jobs, school, or to the yard. You have to shake down a certain number of cells for contraband [smuggled items], buck [homemade alcohol], and shanks [hand-made knives]. Each day has the same cleanup duties, which are done by your building's porter.

Q: *What are the keys to success to being a correctional officer?*

A: That depends on which state you are looking to become a corrections officer in. The state of Michigan requires an associate's degree. I had to take a video test. They also have a physical agility test, such as a required number of push-ups in a certain amount of time, sit-ups, and three sets of stairs where you have to run up and down each set of stairs 60 times. The first set of stairs are 1 inch in height, the second set are 6 inches in height, and the last set of stairs are 13 inches. Some other states require a run of two miles in a certain amount of time. I suggest you find out what your state's requirements are. The college here has a specific correctional officer's training course.

Escort inmates during transfers. You might transport prisoners from one facility to another or accompany them to court appearances. You might also have to restrain inmates in hand-cuffs and leg irons to escort them to and from cells to see visitors.

Search inmates' living quarters. Correctional officers sometimes must search inmates and their living quarters for smuggled goods such as weapons or drugs. You will also have to settle disputes between inmates.

Start Preparing Now

- Keep a job. Because the turnover rate for correctional officers is high, employers like to see that you can stick with a job. Two years of work experience would be a good amount.

 Watch a video about career paths for correctional officers.

- Get a job in a related field. The Federal Bureau of Prisons re-quires entry-level correctional officers to have a college diploma or three years of full-time experience in a field providing counseling, assistance, or supervision to individuals.

Training and How to Get It

The federal, state, or local departments of corrections will provide the specialized training you will need for a position as a correctional officer. This training is based on guidelines set by the American Correctional Association and the American Jail Association. Some states have regional training academies that they "lend" to local agencies. Academy trainees usually receive instruction in a number of subjects, including institutional policies, regulations, and operations. They also study custody and security procedures, legal restrictions, and interpersonal relations. Different systems require different levels of training in firearms use and self-defense skills.

New federal correctional officers must complete three weeks of specialized training at the Federal Bureau of Prisons residential training center at Glynco, Georgia. This training must take place within 60 days of an applicant's appointment. Federal correctional officers also receive 200 hours of formal training within the first year of employment.

Besides formal training, you will probably receive several weeks or months of on-the-job training. This will take place in an actual job setting under the supervision of an experienced officer. On-the-job training varies widely from agency to agency. You might receive training in basic skills, including cell search, body search, transportation of prisoners, supervision of inmates, and human relations. The first year or two of employment is known as a probationary period. At that time, correctional officers may rotate among various assignments and different shifts.

Training continues even when you have worked as a correctional officer for several years. There's always something new to learn. Experienced employees receive additional training as part of an ongoing program to improve job performance.

Learn the Lingo

Here are a few words you might hear as a correctional officer:

- **Agitator** An inmate who manipulates other inmates into fights simply for the sake of enjoyment.

- **Bean slot** A small opening in the cell doors of most segregation areas. It is used to handcuff the inmate before opening the cell. It is also used to deliver the food tray to the inmate without having to open the cell door.

- **Catch a pair** An instruction to a group of inmates to stand in pairs in order to count or control them.

- **Lockdown** In a lockdown, a large group of inmates is held in their cells for a period of time. A lockdown often follows a major disturbance and sometimes lasts for the entire day or even longer.

- **Slammed** When correctional officers use force to wrestle an inmate to the ground.

Finding a Job

Most correctional institutions require officers to be at least 18 years of age, a U.S. citizen, and free of any felony convictions. A high school education or its equivalent is usually required. Many employers use standardized tests to determine if you are suited to work in a correctional institution. It is crucial that correctional officers have good judgment and the ability to think and act quickly. You'll also be screened for drug use and subject to background and physical fitness checks.

In most states, the position of correctional officer is a civil service position. Applications to take a civil service exam may be accepted continuously. If you pass the examination, you'll be placed on an eligible list according to your ranking. Appointments to correctional officer are made from this list, which remains in effect for about two years.

Tips for Success

- Be an amateur psychologist. Each inmate is different and needs to be treated as an individual. Think carefully about each person you encounter and try to pick out a technique that will be most effective in dealing with that person.

LEARN MORE ONLINE

AMERICAN CORRECTIONAL ASSOCIATION (ACA)
The ACA, founded in 1870, is the oldest and largest correctional association in the world. They provide certification, professional development, conferences, and other information about correctional officers. http://www.aca.org

FEDERAL BUREAU OF PRISONS
The Federal Bureau of Prisons site has information on entrance requirements, training, and career opportunities for correctional officers at the federal level. http://www.bop.gov

OFFICE OF PERSONNEL MANAGEMENT
This is the U.S. federal government's official employment site, which includes openings for correctional officers. https://www.usajobs.gov/

▲ A correctional officer stands at the receiving window to check in new inmates.

- Be a peacemaker. Correctional officers need to be skilled at defusing potentially violent situations. Look for opportunities to help others settle their differences through discussion and negotiation.

Reality Check

Working in a correctional institution can be stressful and dangerous. Every year, some correctional officers are injured in fights with inmates. In addition, correctional officers often suffer from depression because of the bleak working environment and the boredom of their job.

Related Jobs to Consider

Police officer or detective. The jobs that precede the correctional officer's work, police and detectives maintain law and order, prevent crime, and arrest offenders.

Probation officer and parole officer. These positions are all related to corrections work. They monitor and counsel offenders and evaluate their progress in rejoining mainstream society.

Security guard. Security guards protect people and property against theft, vandalism, illegal entry, and fire.

How to Move Up

- Receive a promotion. With education, experience, and training, qualified officers may advance to the position of correctional sergeant, lieutenant, and captain. Ambitious and qualified correctional officers can advance to supervisory positions all the way up to warden.

- Work on an associate's degree. Your chances of promotion will increase if you take some classes at a community college. A bachelor's degree would be even better.

- Volunteer for the dirty work. There are a lot of nasty jobs and shifts in correctional work. There is no better way to get on your supervisor's good side than by taking the New Year's Eve shift.

TEXT-DEPENDENT QUESTIONS

1. *What is the average pay for correctional officers?*

2. *What is a typical day like?*

3. *What are some alternative jobs you could consider?*

4. *How might you move up in this field?*

RESEARCH PROJECTS

1. *The U.S. justice system is complex and, at times, controversial. Educate yourself about about the big picture by reading reports at the Prison Policy Institute (https://www.prisonpolicy.org/) and Correctional Officer.org (http://www.correctionalofficer.org/).*

2. *Make getting in shape your next project. Correctional officers usually have to pass tests in physical fitness, eyesight, and hearing. It helps to be in good shape because the job requires a great deal of walking and standing. If you can work out or join a gym, that's great—but if not, there are lots of free or cheap apps that you can use to design and guide your workouts.*

Firefighter

Help save lives and property. Perform strenuous and challenging work. Work in a team environment.

6

WORDS TO UNDERSTAND

battalion chief: an officer in a fire department's organizational structure.

hazmat: short for "hazardous materials," or substances that are highly flammable or poisonous.

regulations: government rules for activities such as how buildings are constructed.

Every year, fires kill thousands of people and cause billions of dollars in property damage. Firefighters help protect people against these dangers by responding to a variety of emergencies, from home and factory fires to traffic accidents. Although there is a lot of "waiting-around" time in the firefighting business, when an emergency arises, these professionals have to move fast and perform exhausting work—pumping water from high-pressure hoses, climbing ladders, breaking through walls, and carrying people to safety.

Becoming a firefighter trainee is the first step in a career in firefighting. Trainees are usually eligible for promotion to firefighter after about a year or two on probation. Some programs require as many as four years as a trainee.

◀ **Firefighters undergo hundreds of hours of training to ensure the safety of themselves, their team, and those that may be in danger.**

According to the National Fire Protection Association, about 69 percent of firefighters in the United States are volunteers. However, there is no shortage of paid positions. In 2016, more than 327,000 people worked in paid firefighting occupations.

Is This the Right Job for You?

To find out if being a firefighter is a good fit for you, read each of the following questions and answer "Yes" or "No."

Yes	No	**1.**	*Do you like working closely with other people?*
Yes	No	**2.**	*Can you think quickly under pressure?*
Yes	No	**3.**	*Do you have good stamina?*
Yes	No	**4.**	*Can you tolerate working outside in difficult weather conditions?*
Yes	No	**5.**	*Can you remain calm in emergencies?*
Yes	No	**6.**	*Can you perform a variety of complicated tasks?*
Yes	No	**7.**	*Are you unfazed by heights, slippery surfaces, or dense smoke?*
Yes	No	**8.**	*Can you perform well in a job that requires bending, running, squatting, pulling, and climbing?*
Yes	No	**9.**	*Can you use your experience and judgment to plan and accomplish goals?*
Yes	No	**10.**	*Can you lift and carry heavy objects and materials?*

If you answered "Yes" to most of these questions, you might consider a career as a firefighter. To find out more about this job, read on.

What's the Work Like?

A firefighter, obviously, puts out fires. During duty hours, you have to be prepared to respond immediately to a fire or any other emergency that arises. At every incident, you'll work as part of a team performing specific duties assigned by a superior officer, usually a **battalion chief** or fire captain.

However, there is more to the job than spraying water on buildings. Most calls to which firefighters respond involve medical emergencies, and about two-thirds of all fire departments provide emergency medical service. You might put out a fire, treat injuries, or perform other vital functions, such as cardiopulmonary resuscitation (CPR).

In addition, some firefighters work in **hazmat** units. They are trained to control, prevent, and clean up materials such as oil spills. Firefighters also perform rescues using ropes and associated hardware and power tools. They also assist in fire prevention, public relations, and educational activities; operate firefighting equipment; and perform routine station and equipment maintenance.

TALKING MONEY

The average annual wage for firefighters in 2016 was $48,030. Working more than 40 hours a week is not uncommon; firefighters can earn overtime for working extra shifts. They also receive excellent benefits, including medical insurance, vacation and sick leave, and pension plans. Most career firefighters are members of a union, such as the International Association of Firefighters.

▲ A team of firefighter trainees hoists a dummy (simulating a fire rescue victim) from the second story of a building.

In large fire departments, a trainee might be instructed for several weeks at the department's academy. Training programs usually combine formal classroom instruction with on-the-job training under the supervision of experienced firefighters. You will study firefighting techniques, fire prevention, chemical hazards, local building codes, and emergency medical procedures. You'll learn how to use axes, chainsaws, fire extinguishers, and ladders. You will also respond to simulated fire alarms and practice various techniques during training fires.

After successfully completing this course, the trainees are assigned to a fire company, where they undergo a period of probation. Firefighters under probation usually perform the same duties as regular firefighters, although they might participate in some additional training sessions and practice drills.

TALKING TRENDS

Thanks to construction regulations and technological improvements, fires occur far less frequently than they did in the past. However, firefighting jobs will probably continue to grow as suburban areas convert volunteer firefighting positions to paid positions. Competition for firefighting jobs is keen.

Who's Hiring?

- City or county fire departments (About 9 out of every 10 firefighters work here.)

- Specific state or federal units, such as airports

- Private firefighting companies

Where Are the Jobs?

Firefighting takes place both inside and outside in all possible weather conditions. Firefighters work in a variety of settings, including urban and suburban areas, national forests and parks, airports, chemical plants, industrial sites, and rural areas, such as grasslands and forests. They frequently have to work in high places, on slippery surfaces, and around dust, dirt, smoke, heat, chemicals, and odors. Some large cities have thousands of paid firefighters, while many small towns have only a few.

Firefighters spend much of their time at fire stations, which often resemble college dormitories. They share cooking duties and shop for groceries as a team. If they receive

▲ Firefighters are sometimes called to help with rescue efforts that don't deal with fire. Here, firefighters undergo ice rescue training.

a call while they are in the store, they'll have to drop their bags and go. When an alarm sounds, firefighters respond rapidly, regardless of the weather or the time.

Firefighters work strange hours. Many work a 24-on/48-off shift. This means that firefighters report to work at 8 a.m. the day of their shift and continue working until 8 a.m. the following morning. Then they might have the following two days off (48 hours). In other departments, firefighters work a day shift of 10 hours for three or four days, a night shift of 14 hours for three or four nights, have a few days off, and then repeat the cycle. Firefighters also work regular shifts on holidays and weekends.

A Typical Day

Here are the highlights of a typical day as a firefighter trainee.

Waiting for an alarm. A lot of firefighting involves waiting. Between alarms, firefighters clean and maintain equipment, conduct practice drills and fire inspections, and participate in physical fitness activities. They also prepare written reports on fire and emergency incidents.

NOTES FROM THE FIELD

Firefighter trainee, Buffalo, New York

Q: *How did you get your job?*

A: I began working as a paramedic with my local volunteer ambulance corps in college. I really enjoyed saving lives, and I realized I dealt with stressful and life-threatening situations well. After I graduated, I worked as a paramedic while doing my master's, but a lot of it was just routine transports, bureaucracy, and boredom. I looked into joining my local fire department, signed up, and never looked back.

Q: *What do you like best about your job?*

A: The camaraderie with the other firefighters in my hall but most of all saving lives and making a difference.

Q: *What is the most challenging part of the job?*

A: Anything can happen, from cats in trees to car accidents to pulling people out of their burning homes.

Q: *What are the keys to success to being a firefighter trainee?*

A: Be strong—there's a lot of gear to carry. Have a good technical mind, since there's a lot of sophisticated equipment to use. Work well with others, both giving and taking orders. Also be aware of everything around you—a fire is no time to be a space cadet.

Respond to a fire alarm. At a fire, firefighters connect hose lines to hydrants and operate pumps to send water to high-pressure hoses. They also place ladders in order to deliver water to the fire and possibly rescue victims. A firefighter's duties may change several times while the company is in action.

Respond to an emergency. Most calls to firefighters involve medical emergencies. Firefighters are usually the first emergency personnel at the scene of a traffic accident or medical emergency. They may have to treat injuries or perform other vital functions, such as emergency first aid.

Start Preparing Now

- Be physically fit. Applicants with the best opportunities are those who are physically fit and score the highest on physical conditioning and written exams.

- Work hard in school. Most firefighting positions begin with a civil service exam. Good grades also reflect well on you in an interview.

- Take a class at a community college. People who do not have some firefighter education or an emergency medical technician (EMT) certification are at a disadvantage.

- Join a volunteer fire department. It gives you a good background in the profession and shows that you are serious about firefighting.

Training and How to Get It

To apply for a firefighting job, you usually have to pass a written, physical, and medical examination. The minimum age for applying varies between 18 and 21. Most trainee positions require a high school diploma or its equivalent. In recent years, many firefighting positions have begun requiring some post–high school education.

Experience is also a factor. Some employers would like to see a trainee with a year or two in the firefighting field. Obviously, any experience working as a volunteer firefighter would give an applicant an advantage. Knowledge of hand tools used in the construction industry is also considered helpful. Of course, a current driver's license is essential.

The written exam is usually in a multiple-choice format. It tests areas such as reading comprehension, mathematics, map reading, and mechanical skill. This test is important, so it pays to study hard in school. Physical exams test your ability to perform job-specific tasks, such as raising a ladder, carrying a hose, carrying a body, or climbing a truck ladder. Most medical examinations now include drug screening. Firefighters also may be checked on a random basis for drug use after accepting employment.

Almost all fire departments now require firefighters to be certified as EMTs. Most fire departments require the lowest level of certification, known as EMT-Basic. However, larger departments in big cities are increasingly requiring paramedic certification. Some departments include this training in the fire academy. Others prefer that recruits have EMT certification before they apply, but they may give a trainee up to one year to acquire certification on his or her own.

Firefighters have to make quick decisions in emergencies. Some personal qualities that firefighters need to do this are difficult to acquire through training. Firefighters must be alert

▲ Many fire departments require their members to be certified EMTs, which includes CPR certification.

and observant and have self-discipline, courage, and good judgment. You need to decide for yourself if you possess the ability to make a good firefighter.

Learn the Lingo

Here are a few words you'll hear as a firefighter trainee:

- **Back draft** An explosion caused by the sudden rush of oxygen into a room, causing all of the superheated gases to ignite at the same time. A back draft is rare but usually fatal to anyone caught in it.

- **Deck gun** A large water nozzle attached to an engine. Deck guns deliver larger amounts of water than hand-held hoses. They are sometimes called "deluge nozzles."

- **GPM** An abbreviation for "gallons per minute." Firefighters usually put out fires with water. This requires thinking in terms of GPM.

- **Halligan** A steel bar used by firefighters to force their way into build-ings. It is sometimes called a "pro tool." This tool is some-times combined with other forcible entry tools, such as an ax, and referred to as "irons."

See how firefighters are trained.

Finding a Job

You will not usually find an opening for a firefighter position in the "Help Wanted" section of the newspaper or on the Internet. Most cities and counties fill firefighter positions through civil service examinations. Announcements for these tests are often posted in libraries and other government buildings. You can also contact your local fire department to see when the next examination is being given. In addition, local fire departments are a good source of information about a career as a firefighter. The Web sites listed on the right offer links to firefighting jobs throughout the United States.

LEARN MORE ONLINE

U.S. FIRE ADMINISTRATION DEPARTMENT OF HOMELAND SECURITY
This National Fire Academy site provides information about professional qualifications and degree programs in fire science or fire prevention. https://www.usfa.fema.gov/training/nfa/

FIREHOUSE.COM
Almost everything you want to know about firefighting, featuring news and extensive links. http://www.firehouse.com

INTERNATIONAL ASSOCIATION OF FIRE FIGHTERS
A wide-ranging, union-sponsored site that provides information about a career as a firefighter as well as firefighting news. http://www.iaff.org

Tips for Success

- Be a team player. Members of a firefighting crew live closely together. They work under conditions of stress and danger for long periods. It is important to be dependable and able to get along well with others.

- Keep up your strength and speed. You may spend much of your shift just waiting around, but when the alarm sounds you must be ready for action. Use those quiet hours to keep fit.

Reality Check

While firefighters are often regarded as heroes by the public, the work they do is not glamorous. It involves physical and mental stress and long, irregular hours. The job alternates long periods of boredom with the real risk of death or injury from sudden cave-ins of floors, toppling walls, and exposure to flames and smoke. As a long-term career, firefighting is not for everyone.

▲ A firefighter is not always out fighting fires. A lot of the job includes sitting around, waiting for a call or maintaining the trucks and building. Here, a firefighter cleans the truck after returning from a call.

Related Jobs to Consider

Emergency medical technician (EMT). EMTs perform prehospital medical procedures in incidents such as automobile accidents, heart attacks, drownings, and gunshot wounds. It is a firefighter's job without the fires.

Police officer. Like firefighters, police and detectives respond to emergencies and save lives.

Dispatcher. Do you want the excitement of emergency work without the danger? Then try being a dispatcher. It is an absolutely crucial job, but a burning building will not fall on you.

How to Move Up

- Take lots of tests. Firefighting has a chain of command. The line of promotion is typically to engineer, lieutenant, captain, battalion chief, assistant chief, deputy chief, and, finally, chief. To move up to these higher-level positions, firefighters usually take written examinations. Constant studying of techniques and procedures comes in handy. You can take classes at a local community college.

- Do a good job. Job performance is always a factor in moving up.

- Get along with your coworkers. Firefighting is a social profession.

- Earn a degree. For promotion to higher positions, many fire departments now require an associate's degree or even a bachelor's degree. The best fields are fire science or public administration.

TEXT-DEPENDENT QUESTIONS

1. *What is the position of trainee and why is it important?*

2. *Why do firefighters need medical training?*

3. *What does a hazmat unit do?*

4. *What are some related careers you might consider?*

RESEARCH PROJECTS

1. *Get some basic first-aid training. The experience will not only help you get a head start on the medical training you'll need, but you'll also find out if helping others in this way is the kind of career you want. If your local recreation center offers first-aid course, be sure to sign up. If not, explore the Web site of the American Red Cross to find out about opportunities near you (https://www.redcross.org/take-a-class).*

2. *Call your local fire department (do not call 911, though; call the main office number) and ask if someone will meet with you and talk to you about becoming a firefighter. You may be able to schedule a tour of the station where you can meet some people who do this tough job every day. Ask what they like and dislike most about their jobs, what kind of training they had, and what a typical day is like.*

Dispatcher

Keep cool in a crisis. Help save lives.
Assist your community.

7

WORDS TO UNDERSTAND

empathy: the ability to understand the feelings of others.

isolated: here, describes a feeling of loneliness.

turnover: refers to the rate at which workers leave jobs and new ones are hired.

Police, fire, and ambulance dispatchers are the crucial link between the discovery of an incident and the official response to that incident. These dispatchers, who are sometimes also called "911 dispatchers" or, more formally, "public safety telecommunicators," receive reports from people about crimes and emergencies. They then broadcast orders to police units, fire trucks, or ambulances to go to the area of the complaint to investigate and help.

Police, fire, and emergency medical professionals are the first people the public contacts when emergency assistance is required. But it is the dispatcher working behind the scenes who makes sure that help is delivered quickly to where it is needed. The work of dispatchers can be very hectic and stressful. Sometimes many calls for assistance come in at the same time. Sometimes callers get excited, angry, or abusive. Nonetheless,

◄ **A police dispatcher forwards a call about a domestic dispute to the closest unit.**

dispatchers must keep a level head and get the job done. In 2016, there were almost 100,000 police, fire, and ambulance dispatchers in the United States, according to the U.S. Bureau of Labor Statistics.

Is This the Right Job for You?

To find out if being an emergency dispatcher is a good fit for you, read each of the following questions and answer "Yes" or "No."

Yes	No	**1.**	*Do you have excellent communication skills?*
Yes	No	**2.**	*Can you work well under extreme pressure?*
Yes	No	**3.**	*Can you maintain a professional attitude in difficult circumstances?*
Yes	No	**4.**	*Do you consider yourself dependable, reliable, and responsible?*
Yes	No	**5.**	*Can you keep your cool, even in difficult situations?*
Yes	No	**6.**	*Are you detail oriented?*
Yes	No	**7.**	*Do you speak clearly?*
Yes	No	**8.**	*Are you usually good natured and cooperative?*
Yes	No	**9.**	*Are you a good listener?*
Yes	No	**10.**	*Do you have **empathy** for others?*

If you answered "Yes" to most of these questions, you might consider a career as a public safety dispatcher. To find out more about this job, read on.

What's the Work Like?

As a police, fire, or ambulance dispatcher, you will schedule and dispatch people, equipment, or vehicles to carry materials or passengers. Dispatchers keep track of the vehicles that they monitor and control and the actions that they take. You will have to record information about each call and then

TALKING MONEY

Police, fire, and ambulance dispatchers receive higher salaries than dispatchers who work with trucks or taxicabs. That is because public safety dispatchers have extra responsibility. According to the Bureau of Labor Statistics, they make $18.69 an hour on average, or $38,870 a year. That figure usually includes attractive health and retirement benefits.

prepare a report on all activities that occurred during your shifts. You must be able to deal with sudden floods of calls, as well as disruptions caused by bad weather, road construction, or accidents.

As a dispatcher, you will most likely work as part of a team. You might question each caller carefully to determine the type, seriousness, and location of the emergency. Then you'll observe alarm registers and scan maps to determine whether a specific emergency is in the area. The request for help is sent to supervisors. They determine the priority of the incident, the kind and number of units needed, and the location of the closest units. You would then send response units to the scene and monitor the activity of the people answering the dispatched message.

Being a dispatcher can be nerve-racking. The wrong response, or even a slow one, can result in a serious injury or death. Even worse, anxious and fearful callers may become excited

▲ A fire dispatch team monitors the console.

and fail to provide needed information. They may even start yelling at you. Yet despite it all, you must remain calm and in control.

Some dispatchers are certified for emergency medical services. They may provide medical instruction to people on the scene of the emergency until the medical staff arrives. They also give updates on the patient's condition to the ambulance personnel and link the hospital's medical staff to the EMTs in the ambulance.

Who's Hiring?

- State and local governments—mainly with police and fire departments

- Hospitals that dispatch ambulances

- Private ambulance or security companies

Where Are the Jobs?

Police, fire, and ambulance dispatchers work in many different settings, such as a police station, fire station, or hospital. However, in some communities, one central communications center provides all three functions. In other places, the police department operates as the communications center and receives all emergency calls. At the police department, a dispatcher handles the police calls and screens the others before transferring them to the correct service.

Dispatching jobs can be found throughout the country, but most dispatchers work in urban areas at large communications centers. Dispatchers are usually assigned a

TALKING TRENDS

The number of public safety dispatchers will probably continue to grow in the near future. Aging baby boomers are expected to increase the demand for emergency service providers, especially ambulance dispatchers. A high turnover in this stressful job also makes it likely that jobs will always be available.

specific territory and are responsible for all communications within that area. Many dispatchers work in teams.

Whether working alone or in groups, dispatchers sometimes feel **isolated** and stressed out. As a dispatcher, you will be sitting for long periods using telephones, computers, and two-way radios. Dispatchers spend much of their time viewing monitors and observing traffic patterns at video terminals. Most work with state-of the-art electronics. Even smaller departments in rural areas have used federal antiterrorism money to buy better 911 service and in-car computers.

Dispatchers usually work a 40-hour week. However, you have to be willing to be flexible about working hours. After all, someone has to be on duty on evenings, weekends, and holidays.

A Typical Day

Here are the highlights of a typical shift for a dispatcher.

Receive incoming calls. People will call regarding emergency and nonemergency police, fire, and ambulance service. You have to provide information for all calls, even nonemergency ones.

Deal with emergency calls. You will have to question callers to determine their location and the nature of their problem. After analyzing the situation, you or someone else will decide on the response. You will then dispatch the proper units. You will also relay information and messages to and from emergency sites and to law enforcement agencies and hospitals.

Keep a log. A dispatcher usually keeps a detailed record of calls, dispatches, and messages. In addition, you will maintain all files of information relating to emergency calls.

Start Preparing Now

- Be familiar with computers. Knowledge of electronic office equipment is almost a prerequisite for the job. People with computer skills and experience have a much better chance at getting a job as a public safety dispatcher.

- Brush up on your keyboarding. Rare is the dispatching job that does not require typing, filing, record keeping, and other clerical skills.

▲ A 911-dispatcher sends a team of firefighters out to a house fire.

Training and How to Get It

The nice thing about becoming an entry-level dispatcher is that most jobs require nothing more than a high school diploma. Some previous work-related skills, knowledge, or experience might help you get a job in the first place. However, it is not required.

Watch this discussion about what it takes to be an emergency dispatcher.

Dispatchers usually develop the necessary skills on the job. This training can last anywhere from several days to a few months depending on the difficulty of the job. New employees

NOTES FROM THE FIELD

Police dispatcher, Baltimore, Maryland

Q: *How did you get your job?*

A: I was fed up with retail jobs so I set my mind on getting a "real" job. I found the job listed on the Internet, went to the city HR [human resources] office to get the application, then went through a very extensive background check and application process. It was about three months from when I turned my application in to when the chief said, "You're hired. When can you start?"

Q: *What do you like best about your job?*

A: The pay is good and the benefits are awesome. I work with some good people. My job security and pay increases are pretty much guaranteed.

Q: *What is the most challenging part of your job?*

A: You never really know what you're going to get when you answer the phone. There are calls for information: [You] either answer the question or refer the call to someone who can. Then there are calls for service: The caller needs to talk to a police officer. Most of these calls really are unnecessary. There's a specific series of questions to ask every caller to figure out what they need, [and you] put it all in the CAD [computer-aided dispatch] system, key up the radio, and send the cop for that sector. Of course you have officer-initiated calls, traffic stops, warrant and summons service, etc. Your day can be boring for four hours then crazy for the next 30 minutes.

Q: *What are the keys to success to being a dispatcher?*

A: This is not a job for everyone. Patience, the ability to multitask, listen, and speak clearly, I'd say, are essential. I cannot stress enough the importance of being honest in every step of the application process. You will be fingerprinted, and those prints will be checked with the FBI. Your former employers and roommates will be asked to provide references. You will have a cursory physical, drug screen, and in some agencies a polygraph.

usually monitor calls with an experienced dispatcher. They learn how to operate different types of communications equipment, including telephones, radios, and various wireless devices. They learn how to use specific computer software systems. As trainees gain confidence, they begin to handle calls on their own. Even after they are experienced, dispatchers participate in training programs sponsored by their employer.

Many public safety dispatchers receive training in stress and crisis management as well as family counseling. This training helps them to provide effective services to others. At the same time, it helps them manage the stress involved in their work.

There are no licensing or certification requirements to work as a dispatcher. It is a field that is still not heavily regulated by the government. However, some states require that public safety dispatchers possess a certificate to work on a state network, such as the Police Information Network.

Learn the Lingo

Here are a few words you'll hear as a dispatcher:

- **The house** A police station house or home base.

- **Loo** Affectionate slang for a "lieutenant."

- **Open carrier** A police officer or vehicle with an open radio. This tells everyone to be careful about what they say because someone may be listening in.

- **White shirts** A term for lieutenants and higher-ranked personnel, who wear white uniform shirts.

- **10-4** A radio code that means the message has been received: "Gotcha, over and out."

- **10-59** A radio code that indicates an alarm for a fire—the sender of the alarm would still specify the type and location of the fire.

Finding a Job

You can find information on job opportunities for public safety dispatchers from personnel offices of state and local governments. Police departments also have this information. Another possible source of information is the state employment office.

The jobs of police, fire, emergency medical, and ambulance dispatching are often civil service positions. This means you probably need to take a test, called a civil service examination, in order to get the job. Candidates then are placed on a list based on their test scores. Applicants will be called according to the list as openings arise. You also may have to pass an oral exam and a performance test and submit to an interview.

LEARN MORE ONLINE

ASSOCIATION OF PUBLIC SAFETY COMMUNICATIONS OFFICIALS
This union-sponsored site provides information on training and certification for police, fire, and emergency dispatchers. https://www.apcointl.org/

INTERNATIONAL MUNICIPAL SIGNAL ASSOCIATION
An organization that promotes itself as "the leading international resource for information, education and certification for public safety." http://www.imsasafety.org

Tips for Success

- Keep calm. You're not out there at the site of the emergency. Everyone is depending on the coolness and logic of your response. Separate your emotions from the job at hand.

- Listen carefully. People who call 911 may be too upset to communicate clearly. You must listen very closely and ask each caller the right questions to get all the information you need to help that person.

Reality Check

Dispatching is stressful. Dispatchers are involved in tense incidents where there may be a loss of life. In addition, dispatchers can develop eye and back problems from working for long stretches with computers and other electronic equipment.

Related Jobs to Consider

Ticket agent and travel clerk. These occupations also involve directing and controlling the movement of vehicles, freight, and personnel, as well as distributing information and messages.

Emergency medical technician. If you think the switchboard is too far away from the action, remember that EMTs get to ride right in the ambulance.

Nonemergency dispatcher. Do you think there's too much stress in public-safety dispatching? Switch over to dispatching tow trucks, trucks, taxicabs, or gas and electric personnel.

How to Move Up

- Apply for a higher-paying administrative job. If you work hard, you can become a shift supervisor or chief of communications.

- Become a firefighter or a police officer. Why sit behind a desk when you can really get close to the action? Trainee positions often require nothing more than a high school diploma.

- Attend training classes. Training classes can lead to advanced certification and improve your chances for career advancement. Or you can earn an associate's or bachelor's degree.

TEXT-DEPENDENT QUESTIONS

1. *About how many emergency dispatchers are there in the United States?*

2. *Where do emergency dispatchers work?*

3. *What does 10-59 mean?*

4. *How might you move up in this career?*

RESEARCH PROJECTS

1. *Take a course in first aid or CPR. Public safety dispatchers are constantly dealing with medical emergencies. It gives you an advantage if you have any certification for emergency medical services.*

2. *Find out more about what a typical day is like. Check out first-person testimonials like "A Day in the Life of a 911 Dispatcher" (http://sanfranciscopolice.org/day-life-911-dispatcher) and "Career Spotlight: What I Do as a 911 Dispatcher" (https://lifehacker.com/career-spotlight-what-i-do-as-a-911-dispatcher-1749942094).*

▲ An emergency dispatcher must keep calm, and listen carefully. Everyone is depending on you keeping your cool and giving logical responses.

Transportation Security Screener

8

Prevent terrorism. Protect property. Save lives.

WORDS TO UNDERSTAND

disruptive: badly behaved.

microexpressions: small, unintentional changes in someone's facial expression that may reveal what they are really thinking.

temperament: personality.

Airport security jobs are homeland security jobs. That means that U.S. national security depends to some degree on doing them properly. Working as a transportation security screener (also called an airport security screener) is not like being on the assembly line or working at the mall. You are responsible for identifying dangerous objects in baggage, in cargo, or on passengers. It is your job to prevent those objects from being carried onto aircraft. In this sense, screeners are crucial to the prevention of terrorism.

More than 42,000 airport security screeners spend each day scanning people and their luggage to look for things that might, for example, explode. Yet screeners often receive criticism from some of the very people they are trying to protect: impatient travelers frustrated by long lines

◀ **A transportation security screener manually inspects a passenger's luggage to remove any contraband items or to check for items that were unclear on the X-ray machine.**

and changing security requirements. Security screeners have to maintain their concentration and professional bearing despite these challenges.

Is This the Right Job for You?

To find out if being a transportation security screener is a good fit for you, read each of the following questions and answer "Yes" or "No."

Yes	No	**1.**	*Can you lift 70-pound bags?*
Yes	No	**2.**	*Can you handle the challenge of looking for weapons and explosive devices?*
Yes	No	**3.**	*Can you maintain a professional attitude in difficult circumstances?*
Yes	No	**4.**	*Do you consider yourself dependable, reliable, and responsible?*
Yes	No	**5.**	*Can you stay calm, even in difficult situations?*
Yes	No	**6.**	*Are you conscientious about paperwork?*
Yes	No	**7.**	*Do you have excellent communication skills?*
Yes	No	**8.**	*Can you work flexible hours?*
Yes	No	**9.**	*Can you stand for four hours without a break?*
Yes	No	**10.**	*Are you sensitive to other people's needs and feelings?*

If you answered "Yes" to most of these questions, you might consider a career as a transportation security screener. To find out more about this job, read on.

What's the Work Like?

As the job title suggests, an airport security screener must screen all passengers and carry-on luggage at an airport. If an explosive device gets past you, then it is getting on the plane. As a transportation security screener, you will be responsible for passenger safety. You will also look for possible signs of trouble at security checkpoints.

TALKING MONEY

Transportation security officers receive an average of $39,680 per year, according to 2016 data from the U.S. Bureau of Labor Statistics. They are paid between $16 to $22 an hour. Opportunities for overtime work are usually plentiful. Employees of the federal government usually receive excellent benefits and pensions.

Most airport checkpoints have at least two or three screeners working on the job. One person monitors the X-ray equipment used to scan the carry-on items. Another makes sure the walkthroughs are going smoothly. If the X-ray attendant sees something suspicious, she or he alerts a screener. The screener then goes to the conveyor belt and identifies the owner of

▲ As backpacks, laptops, purses, and other items move on a conveyor belt in front of an X-ray machine, transportation security screeners keep an eye out for any illegal substances, firearms, or other deadly weapons.

the bag. They go to a table alongside the checkpoint, and the screener physically inspects the baggage. Screeners in the property search patrol may also use handheld metal detectors or occasionally perform personal "pat down" searches on passengers. They might also use an explosives-trace-detection machine to test carry-on bags for the smallest particles of explosives. Screeners do not have the power to arrest suspects but must work with airport police if they suspect a crime has been committed. Airport security screening work is sometimes boring. However, you will rotate frequently among the various duties, and you will probably be too busy to doze.

TALKING TRENDS

The fear of terrorism increases the desire for increased transportation security. However, advances in the technology of screening will make it possible for the job to be done with fewer people in the future. In general, hiring for airport security screeners should remain fairly stable.

Where Are the Jobs?

Not surprisingly, transportation security officers mainly work in airports. Some work as baggage security screeners. They search checked luggage for explosives and do not have to interact with the public. Most officers, however, work at security checkpoints located before the boarding gates in all airport terminals.

An airport checkpoint can be a very stressful environment. You are surrounded by a great deal of noise from alarms, machinery, and people. There are also numerous distractions, time pressures, and **disruptive** passengers. Lines back up and people complain about potentially missed flights. It's a good thing that breaks come regularly—once every two or three hours—and can last up to half an hour.

Find out how airport screening technology works.

Who's Hiring?

- Transportation Security Administration (TSA)

- Private screening companies

A Typical Day

Here are the highlights of a typical day for a transportation security screener.

Staff different stations at the security checkpoint. Each lane at a security checkpoint has different duty stations, such as X-ray, bag check, walk-through metal detector, and handheld metal detector. Screeners rotate to different stations throughout their shift.

Make sure passengers are ready to enter the metal detectors. You will have to relay a series of instructions across a barrier so that no passengers will approach wearing their shoes, coats, or other forbidden things.

Physically inspect baggage and people. Part of your job is to encroach on other people's privacy. This means that you have to rifle through people's bags in search of suspect items spotted by the X-ray operator.

▲ Working for the TSA means ensuring travelers' safety while managing lines of people moving through the security checkpoint.

Deal with angry passengers. Irritated passengers routinely accuse airport screeners of stealing or breaking their cell phones, computers, or cameras. Others will blame you for "making me miss my flight!"

Start Preparing Now

- Get your high school diploma. Transportation security screener is an entry-level job. In most cases, a high school diploma is needed.

- Work at the mall. Even a part-time security job at the mall will give you a feel for this kind of work and look good on your application.

Training and How to Get It

Some experience in security work might help you become an airport security screener. However, your employer will provide all specific training. Before 2001, private employers provided airport security screeners with about 10 hours of classroom instruction and

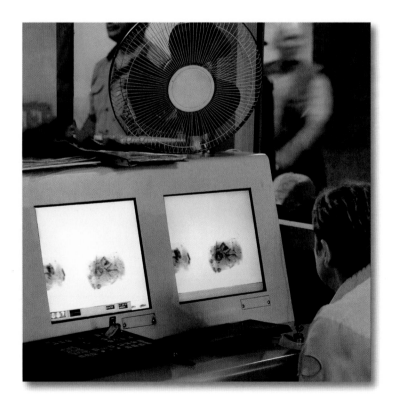

◀ The TSA regularly sends out software to train screeners how to detect weapons inside luggage. The TSA also periodically superimposes images of dangerous items on the contents of bags to make sure screeners are alert.

NOTES FROM THE FIELD

Transportation security screener, Baltimore, Maryland

Q: *How did you get your job?*

A: After the terrorist attacks on September 11, 2001, [the U.S. government created] the Transportation Security Administration (TSA). Before 9/11, screening passengers and their property was handled by the airlines so that different private companies were hired, creating an uneven appearance of security. Often the private screeners were low-paid workers and did not consider their work a career. While nothing that happened on 9/11 was the screeners' fault, it was clear that a better system was needed.

I decided to be a part of the first federal TSA screener workforce at Baltimore-Washington International Airport (now Baltimore-Washington Thurgood Marshall International Airport). BWI was the first in the nation, and it was exciting to serve my country in such a difficult time. After a grueling day of assessments and testing, I was hired and sent to a one-week training course. After I passed the course I started at the airport, and just like that I was a federal passenger screener. I have been with TSA for over five years, and we are now called Transportation Security Officers (TSOs) as a part of the Department of Homeland Security.

Q: *What do you like best about your job?*

A: The most rewarding thing about serving as a TSO is the respect we receive from the passengers and the knowledge that we are a part of history. My favorite part of the job is assisting the passengers, as it can often be stressful for them and at times confusing. Passengers with small children need our assistance, and I try to always greet them with a smile. We are officers, but we do not need to treat the passengers like suspects. They are just simply trying to get to their plane and the business trip or vacation that awaits them. Getting them through with a smile and a sense of security is our mission, and I think we do it pretty well.

Q: *What's the most challenging part of your job?*

A: Creating something new is difficult and very challenging for us and for the public. [After 9/11,] rules were much stricter and the lines were long. But everyone understood the need to be as cautious as possible. We even had a National Guardsman on each checkpoint, and I can assure you that having someone with a machine gun gets everyone's attention.

We must be vigilant and watch for anything out of the ordinary. If something doesn't seem right, it must be checked. We rotate to a different position every 30 minutes so we don't lose concentration. This also allows for a varied day, as it can be extremely busy during one part of the day and extremely slow during another part. Boredom is a challenge, and we must always stay focused.

Q: *What are the keys to success to being a transportation security screener?*

A: Anyone interested in this career must be prepared to meet the rigorous assessment standards and realize that we are serving our country in a sensitive position. Many opportunities exist, but first you must prove that you can handle the pressure and sensitivity and be flexible. This is one job that you may see the news before going to work and know it will be a hard day. That takes the right temperament, and it's not for everybody.

20 to 30 hours of on-the-job training. Because terrorists used airplanes to attack the United States in 2001, the U.S. government became extremely involved in airport security. This led to an increase in training for screeners. They are taught not only to recognize potential threats but also to deal effectively with the public. Screeners must give directions and respond to questions in a reasonable tone and manner. It's not so easy after being asked the same thing 10,000 times.

Once you graduate to working at an airport checkpoint, you will probably work under the supervision of experienced screeners. For example, trainees are not permitted to monitor the X-ray machine unattended, even though they might have had hours of practice in class. However, on-the-job training with a mentor is the best way to learn the tricks of the screening trade. The TSA regularly sends out software to train screeners how to detect weapons inside luggage. The TSA also briefly superimposes images of dangerous items on the contents of bags to make sure screeners are alert. Each year every security screener must pass a difficult recertification exam. Some do not make the grade and move on to other careers. There are also quarterly spot checks and occasional encounters with undercover inspectors. If screeners fail to pass tests, they are sent back to class for remedial training. Despite this training, a split-second distraction is enough to be fired, shut down an entire terminal, cost an airline millions of dollars, or worse.

Learn the Lingo

Here are a few words and abbreviations you'll hear as a transportation security screener:

- **ETD** "Explosive trace detection" equipment reads swabs taken from items to detect trace amounts of explosives.

- **ETP** "The explosive trace portal" is a machine that gives out puffs of air and analyzes for traces of explosives. It's also known as a "puffer" or "puff portal."

▲ Screening travelers includes checking identification.

- **Hinky** A slang term for nervous or jumpy. Screeners use it to mean that they have a vague, intuitive "bad feeling" about something that justifies investigation, but they can't exactly explain why.

- **IED** An "improvised explosive device" can be assembled past security with seemingly harmless parts. IEDs are the reason for the ban on carry-on liquids and gels on commercial aircraft.

- **VAP** "Voluntarily abandoned property" refers to banned items stopped at security checkpoints. The most common are cigarette lighters (37,000 a day in the United States), which are thrown out as hazardous waste.

Finding a Job

An airport security job is usually obtained through the federal government or through private screening companies. When you apply for a job with the government, you must apply for specific airport security jobs currently offered by the TSA. You cannot broadly apply for any airport security job. The TSA lists both part- and full-time openings and provides the necessary forms on its Web site. It takes very little time to fill out the information requested on the application and press the "send" button. In a few weeks you'll hear if you made it past the first round.

To discover if a private screening company hires at an airport at which you want to work, you can contact the airport's human resources department or visit the employment section of its Web site. Sometimes a checkpoint security station contracted out to a private company keeps applications on hand.

No matter how you apply, you will have to answer nosy security-clearance questions. There is usually an interview process and possibly an aptitude test. If you are hired, you will be fingerprinted, photographed, and subjected to a background check and a physical fitness test. You must be 18 years of age and a U.S. citizen or U.S. national to apply. You will also need a high school diploma (or its equivalent) or at least one year of full-time experience in security, aviation screening, or X-ray work.

Tips for Success

- Security with a smile. Transportation security officers have to balance the necessity for airport security with the need for customer service. Security officers are supposed to keep bombs, potential weapons, and terrorists off planes yet smile at total strangers most of the day. You have to be able to screen passengers but not go so far as to make them frustrated or uncomfortable.

- Be observant. As a screener you'll need to spot prohibited items in the confusing jumble of a passenger's luggage. You must also learn to "read" people's faces and body language and report anything that arouses your suspicions.

Reality Check

Many of the nation's federal airport security screeners suffer from understaffing and excessive overtime. In this career, you have to be ready to put in long hours. You also have to like working with others, but maintain an authoritative attitude to search luggage and people.

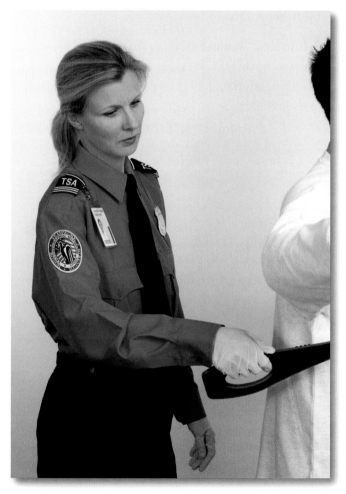

▲ Transportation security screeners must be vigilant and watch for anything out of the ordinary. If something doesn't seem right, it must be checked.

Related Jobs to Consider

Security guard. These people also protect lives and property but often without the pressure of an airport environment.

Police officer. This law enforcement job offers greater rewards and better pay than airport work. However, the personal risks are also greater.

Receptionist. If you enjoy working with the public in a nonconfrontational way, this job might be a good choice.

How to Move Up

LEARN MORE ONLINE

OFFICE OF PERSONNEL MANAGEMENT: USAJOBS
This is the federal government's official employment site, including openings for transportation security officers. https://www.usajobs.gov

TRANSPORTATION SECURITY ADMINISTRATION
The official TSA Web site with information and an employment section. https://www.tsa.gov

AMERICAN FEDERATION OF GOVERNMENT EMPLOYEES (AFGE)
Airport security screeners are represented by the AFGE, the largest federal employee union. This site is the homeland security page of the AFGE Web site. http://www.afge.org

- Advance through the TSA. The TSA is unique among federal employers because it does not use the standard GS grading system. Instead, letters rather than numbers identify TSA grades. Most screeners are hired as D-Bands. They can move up to E-Bands after two years with the TSA and a favorable performance review.

- Specialize. Experienced screeners can switch into programs such as "Bomb Appraisal" and "Screening Passengers by Observation Technique."

- Move within the Department of Homeland Security. Screeners can switch to other security, protection, or law enforcement jobs in the department. Good performance reviews can be your ticket to a different federal job.

- Advance to a management position. It's possible to ascend the chain of command at the TSA through hard work, reliability, and test scores. Managerial jobs are G-, H-, and I-Band positions.

TEXT-DEPENDENT QUESTIONS

1. *What do security screeners do?*

2. *What is the average salary?*

3. *What are some of the down sides to this job?*

4. *What can you do now to prepare yourself for this field?*

RESEARCH PROJECTS

1. *Part of your job will involve assessing strangers to figure out what's on their minds. Find out about body language and microexpressions, start learning how to interpret them. Start with articles like "Body Language vs. Microexpressions" (https://www.psychologytoday.com/blog/spycatcher/201112/body-language-vs-micro-expressions) and "Guide to Reading Microexpressions" (https://www.scienceofpeople.com/guide-reading-microexpressions/).*

2. *Make physical fitness a priority. Airport screeners have one of the federal government's highest rates of job-related injuries, mainly due to hoisting checked luggage and overstuffed carry-ons. If you can join a gym, that's great—but if not, there are lots of apps that will assist you in developing a workout program.*

Becoming a firefighter trainee is the first step in a career in fire-fighting. Trainees are usually eligible for promotion to firefighter after about a year or two on probation. Some programs require as many as four years as a trainee.

INDEX

PHOTO CREDITS